Milton E. Polsky is a professor at the Hunter College Program for Gifted Youth, where he heads the drama program and directs the On-the-Spot Players. He also works with young people and adults as a drama specialist for the New York City Board of Education. A former Shubert Playwriting Fellow, his plays and musicals have been produced off-Broadway and at colleges. He has directed improvisational ensembles for various New York City agencies and is the author of numerous articles, plays, and books.

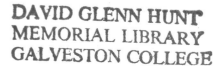

Milton E. Polsky

LET'S IMPROVISE

BECOMING CREATIVE, EXPRESSIVE & SPONTANEOUS THROUGH DRAMA

A SPECTRUM BOOK

PRENTICE-HALL, INC., *Englewood Cliffs, New Jersey 07632*

Library of Congress Cataloging in Publication Data

POLSKY, MILTON E
 Let's improvise.

 (A Spectrum Book)
 Bibliography: p.
 Includes index.
 1. Improvisation (Acting)   I. Title.
 PN2071.I5P65   792'.028   80-10238
 ISBN 0-13-532069-0
 ISBN 0-13-532051-8 pbk.

Editorial/production supervision and
interior design by Carol Smith
Cover design by Yasuo Kubota
Front cover illustration by Marc Rosenthal
Manufacturing buyer: Cathie Lenard

A SPECTRUM BOOK

Printed in the United States of America

10 9 8 7 6 5 4 3 2 1

PRENTICE-HALL INTERNATIONAL, INC., *London*
PRENTICE-HALL OF AUSTRALIA PTY. LIMITED, *Sydney*
PRENTICE-HALL OF CANADA, LTD., *Toronto*
PRENTICE-HALL OF INDIA PRIVATE LIMITED, *New Delhi*
PRENTICE-HALL OF JAPAN, INC., *Tokyo*
PRENTICE-HALL OF SOUTHEAST ASIA PTE. LTD., *Singapore*
WHITEHALL BOOKS LIMITED, *Wellington, New Zealand*

For the three women in my life—
Sarah, Roberta, and Madelyn

CONTENTS

AN INVITATION TO IMPROVISE

Inside us all, there is a powder keg of untapped creativity ready to burst forth into expression—be it writing, cooking, dancing, gardening, singing. The creative act lights up a new way of looking at things, giving life fresh pleasure and meaning.

You are about to begin an exciting journey into the wonderful world of creative drama, in which you can become anyone, anywhere, anytime—through the magic of improvisation.

Read to the end of this paragraph. When you come to the paragraph's last word (*go*), rhyme it with another word, any word that comes immediately to mind. Then stand up and pantomime that word. If the word is *throw,* for example, you could be throwing a balloon to someone, or you could become a balloon being thrown about by the wind. If there is someone else in the room with you, try a *brief* two-character skit centering around the word. At this point, don't think too

You are about to begin an exciting journey into the wonderful world of creative drama, where you can become anyone, anywhere, anytime through the magic of improvisation. The Patchwork Players, under the direction of Milton Polsky and Julie Martin, make a travel machine.
(*Photo by Alex Gersznowicz*)

much or worry about how careful or "correct" the miming is; just do it for fun. Ready? Set? Go!

By doing this simple exercise, you already can sense one important value of improvisational drama—spontaneity. In fact, that is what improvisation means—the spontaneous response to new and unexpected situations under structured circumstances, a way of "letting yourself go" with self-control. By doing even this simple exercise, you have stretched not only your body but your imagination, the magic word that can unlock your creative spirit, enabling you to push out beyond the here and now to discover new worlds of feelings, ideas, and experiences.

Improvisational drama can be experienced almost anywhere—in the classroom, at home, onstage, in summer recreation and drama programs, in churches, hospitals, and rehabilitation settings—and by anyone, from children to senior adults. Players need not be concerned with expensive props or elaborate costumes and stage settings. From "mere" space alone, a marvelous and diverse world of familiar and fantasy activity can be constructed and shared.

Did you rhyme your word with *throw* . . .
(*Photo by Leonard Lewis*)

or perhaps *bow*?
(*Photo by Claudia M. Caruana*)

Whether it is practiced onstage, in the classroom, or during the process of daily living, the goals of improvisational drama are essentially the same—to become more in touch with the body and senses, to express and communicate to others untapped creative potential of the human imagination, and to expand and deepen an awareness of the ordinary as well as the fantastic things in life.

In an open and relaxed atmosphere, you will feel free to create—to transform an "ordinary" idea into a celebration of life; to touch each other, make powerful eye contact, and release strong emotions; to "try on" a variety of characters from life and literature; to test and revise your feelings and thoughts about your immediate environment and beyond.

Through further work in play-making, new roles will be

Improvisation yields exciting possibilities for everyone, from the classroom . . .
(*Photo by Jane Barowitz*)

AN INVITATION TO IMPROVISE

to the recreation program.

(Photo courtesy of Brookdale Drama Project, Milton Polsky, Director)

tried on, old roles reexamined with a new inner freedom. In the process of role-playing and role reversal, you will learn to perceive a problem from another person's point of view. Cooperation among players in discovering, devising, and acting out conflict situations, scenes, and plays further enhances the process of examining your own sense of values.

In the process of doing is the discovery. The plan of the book emphasizes development.

In the beginning stages (the first four chapters), you will discover nonverbal techniques and exercises designed to help you move, think, and create "on your feet" with a free-flowing spontaneity. There then follow two chapters dealing with contrasting varieties of pantomime. The chapter on sono-mime is the transition to verbal improvisations, which comprise the last six chapters.

To deepen an awareness of the ordinary as well as the fantastic things in life. (From *Wings n' Things* by Sharon Doyle.)

(Photo courtesy of Archaesus Productions, Gary Young, Producing Director.)

As you become increasingly aware of your body as a vitally expressive instrument, inner confidence will be fostered. You will have the opportunity to choose from hundreds of exercises that encourage personal and social growth—to change objects into all kinds of surprises; to surprise yourself by actually becoming an object; to tell stories on the spot that other players have to finish; to sing, dance, draw, write poetry; to become someone else's voice; to make up stories using a bag containing totally unrelated, everyday props . . . and more.

As you further discover your creative capabilities and become more aware of others in the group, your ability for verbal expression will be steadily strengthened. The challenge of cooperation through role-playing and play-making is an important theme that runs through the book. All the exercises in this text are nonjudgmental. One player's interpretation is just as valid as another's—and variety and individuality are always encouraged.

To foster personal awareness, the book features "Add Your Own" spaces in which participants—called players—can contribute their original ideas and images. A "Player's Diary" at the end of each chapter is designed to enhance self-discovery further. Feel free to add your own questions, thoughts, and observations. Try variations and spin-offs on games and exercises whenever you can.

Your improvisational journey is about to begin. Players spanning virtually all age levels who have participated in workshops through the years have commented on the tremendous benefits yielded—losing one's inhibitions, building confidence through teamwork, developing freedom to take creative risks, and receiving valuable training in play-making.

We hope you will continue to experiment with the techniques and exercises that follow, letting your imagination take

"Ascent," the final image of an historical collage of humanity's yearning to fly.
(*Photo courtesy of Street 70 Mime Troupe,
directed by Craig Babcock.*)

off and soar into many different kinds of worlds, so that—in the words of Victor Hugo—you may

Be like the bird, who
Pausing in its flight
On limbs too slight,
Feels it give way beneath
Yet sings,
Knowing it hath wings.

ACKNOWLEDGMENTS

Some of the ideas that took final shape in this book first appeared in *Dramatics* magazine and in Westwood Press' *Pandora's Box* (Creata-Play series) coauthored with Joan Gardner.

While the book was still a manuscript, Katharine and Mary Mylenki, Roz McWatters, and Cherie Miller put in hours of expert typing; and Paul Golub, Dale Robert McCausland, and Amanda Udis-Kessler offered invaluable assistance during the final stages of the manuscript's preparation.

When the manuscript arrived at Prentice-Hall, Frank Moorman and Debbie Leitner were always available to answer questions and offer welcome advice. Alice Harvey copyedited the manuscript with perception and care, and Carol Smith gave it such sensitive and sound attention during the production cycle.

All my students, too numerous to thank individually and whose unique talents pervade these pages, have served as an inspiration. The photographs that so beautifully illustrate the text were contributed by many professional, college, and community theater companies, as well as local photographers whose names appear with their photos.

My heartfelt gratitude to all of these people.

Finally, without the support of my family, this book would not have been possible. Thank you, Howard, Jonah, and Madelyn. And special thanks to my wife, Roberta, whose steadfast encouragement and astute editorial eye often saved the day.

LET'S IMPROVISE

Well begun is half done!

Horace

BREAKING THE ICE 1

We all experience some tension during the normal course of our everyday lives. Tension may result from the uncertainty of making decisions, from fear of the unknown, or from pressures to conform to patterns of daily living.

One way to break icy blocks of tension is through warm, friendly group movement and name games. What both non-verbal movement and verbal name games have in common is that they help bring people closer together, which is indispensable for improvisational ensemble acting.

Feel free to follow this sequence of exercises, or select and combine, or rearrange them to best fit the interests and needs of the group.

IMPROVISED MOVEMENT

It is interesting that many figures of speech associated with tension are connected with the body, such as "cold feet," "thick tongue," and "butterflies in the stomach." Think about what happens to that tension when you move your "cold feet" through imaginary, glowing warm sands or fly around as a butterfly or bird, letting your fancy take you where you wish. In other words, you can overcome many of your inner jitters through joyful, spontaneous movement.

START IN A CIRCLE

All the exercises in this chapter start in a circle formation for very good reasons. First of all, the circle gives a welcome sense of security and unity. There is really no beginning or end in a circle, and so everyone is more or less on equal footing. Standing or sitting close to one another usually makes the process of forming friendships easier. There are no "corners" in a circle; this makes eye contact easier. Seeing one another when discussing gound rules of an exercise or how you feel after the exercise helps enhance the process of communication. Because we live in a world bound by so many boxed-in, architectural straight lines, it is refreshing to start off in a circle. Let's begin!

SAY HELLO

1. Everyone join hands in a circle; then drop hands. You're ready to move!

2. To the beat of a drum or music or the clap of hands, walk around the classroom or work space.

3. When the drum stops (or the leader says "freeze!"), reach out, shake hands, and say "hello" or "hi" to your immediate neighbor. (The handshake is probably the most prevalent gesture as a sign of greeting, going back to ancient Greeks and Romans.)

4. When the drum starts again, continue walking around the room in *complete* silence. When the drum stops again (at irregular pauses), say hello to your neighbor with your eyes only (a wink, a blink, etc.); the next time around, say hello with your shoulders, then with your ears, your knees, and so on, until you have "talked" with different parts of your body. Hold a "hand conversation" with your partner. What are the hands like? How do they feel? Send out signals with your arms, and imagine your hands are lights; think in terms of colors that express how you feel inside your torso—your emotional center. No words are necessary; let your body speak for you. How many different ways can you say hello without talking?

How many ways can you say hello without talking?
(*Photo by Leonard Lewis*)

TWIRL YOUR THUMBS, THIGHS, AND TOES

1. Now, to get your motor really racing, stand in place, and twirl your thumbs around each other.

2. Keep them moving, and add the circular motion of your fingers.

3. Add the circular motion of your wrists. One by one, add arms, shoulders, chest, pelvis (spinning inside an imaginary

Hula-Hoop), legs—all the way down to your toes. By this time, your whole body should be in motion.

4. Move around the room, eliminating in reverse order the twirling motions, concentrating on isolating your limbs and other parts of your body.

5. Now stand in place and relax. Shake yourself out like a puppy just coming in from the rain. (If you have something against puppies, substitute your own image.)

6. Breathe evenly through your nose, and exhale. Relax.

7. *In place,* loosen up your body once again, this time in slow, exaggerated steps. Dangle your head from side to side like a floppy mop; bend your torso like a rubber doll. Roll your neck around like a robot—click-click-click. Reach out, and play an imaginary piano; move your legs up and down as in deep snow. Relax. Breathe gently.

MAGIC MOVER

1. Take turns being the Magic Mover. Magic Mover commands the players to "lead" with different parts of their bodies as they move around the room. Leading means that a particular part of the body will prominently stick out, acting almost like a magnet taking the rest of the body with it. Lead first with your head, then your chin, your backside (moving backwards, of course), and other parts of the body.

2. While leading with different parts of the body, move in any order:

forward	in crooked lines
backward	in oblique lines
sideways	in curves
zig-zag	high
in straight lines	low

You can slide, skip, gallop, or slow trot. Creative movement is varied through

speed	rhythm
size	duration

Spontaneity in creative movement through the commands of Magic Mover.
(*Photo courtesy of Archaesus Productions: 1975. Mime Tripping*)

From time to time, the beat should change from single to double beat; change the speed from fast, to medium, to slow. Alternate the beats and speeds for variety. Magic Mover can also assign the players numbers corresponding to different parts of the body, and then call out the numbers, such as "Stretch your ones" (left arms); "Wiggle your twos" (noses); and so forth. It is fun to call out such open-ended commands as "Nod your (<u>head</u>)"; "Twist your (<u>shoulders, neck</u>)"; "Bend your (<u>elbows</u>)." Magic Mover can call out such commands as "Touch nose to knee"; "chin to chest"; "hands to hips"; "heel to heel"; "toes to nose"; "ear to elbow"; etc., as players respond to commands.

3. Magic Mover can command the players to take some magic shrinking pills and become as small as they can, or to take magic expanding pills to become as large as possible. Magic Mover can command players to pick a flower and share it with another person . . . hold it and smell it. Magic Mover can command the players to become kites blowing in the wind, or feathers falling from a hat, or a rubber band stretching, and so on, and so on. Magic Mover varies the commands by saying move *as if* you are

- marching in a parade
- running in a race
- playing hopscotch.

Add your own:

_____

_____

_____

With minimal coaching, you will come up with diverse running, skipping, leaping, and walking movements. Spontaneity in creative movement recalls times when running, skipping, and stretching were common, everyday activities—a natural way of communicating with the world around you.

> *Ask yourself, as a matter of self-evaluation: Have I stretched my body and my mind to come up with the most interesting and varied movements?*

4. Now it is time to relax. Shake yourself out. Imagine you are a block of ice or a candle, and melt to the floor. (You can join hands, lock arms, touch heels to heels, or the like and melt together if you like). Breathe and exhale through your nose. Think of the floor as a magic carpet that can take you anywhere. Trust your own impressions, and give your expression style.

STYLIZED TAG

This is an excellent exercise to illustrate two key improvisational concepts: (1) letting yourself go and (2) self-control. Through doing the exercise, you will feel free to let go of your inhibitions and fears about "performing." With a newly discovered emotion of opening up, release, and relaxation, you will feel freer to concentrate. In turn, this concentration will

Stylized Tag . . . let yourself go.
(*Photo by Rhoda Cohen*)

Stylized Tag . . . with self-control.
(*Photo by Rhoda Cohen*)

enable you to feel more relaxed and free to take creative risks. You will then be able to use the power of concentration to communicate your feelings, thoughts, and ideas in a variety of experiences. You can become whatever the imagination allows.

1. One person is chosen "It."

2. It begins a movement, adding a sound to complement the movement.

3. Everyone imitates this sound and movement, moving away (no running allowed!) from It, who tries to tag another player.

4. When It does tag someone, the new It quickly initiates a new movement and sound. The rest of the players imitate the new It.

5. As a variation, It can become an animal, and the other players become something that the animal would need for food. The player tagged becomes a new animal. Another variation is for It to tag another player with different parts of the body—elbow, knee, toe, head, nose, back, and so forth. Still another variation is for It to tag another player *within five seconds.* In this case, everyone has to cooperate to ensure that the flow does not stop.

6. The exercise continues until everyone has had a chance. Try to stylize the movements and sounds. Avoid wasted energy; find the clean and clear stroke. Search for the difference that makes the difference. Stretch your mind and imagination for interesting movements and sounds.

You are now ready for a challenging and relaxing fantasy trip based on nature—another natural way to begin.

FANTASY TRIP

WATER-WOODS-WINDOW

1. Circle formation. Everyone into the pool! (Don't forget to put on your swimming suit.) Swim and splash around. Mix up your movements as you stretch your head, arms, and legs. Just be yourself as you do anything you want to in the water—water ballet, treading water, water polo. Really feel the water splash all over your body. What areas of your body are most affected by the water in the pool?

2. Suddenly, the mood and place change. The water freezes over, and the pool turns into ice as smooth and slippery as glass. The swimmers now put on their warm clothing and ice skates (take your time). Waltz around the rink; the group can hum a tune, or you can play an appropriate musical accompaniment, such as *The Skater's Waltz* by Macdowell, to enhance the mood. Skating for the first time? A little shaky? Choose a partner! Do figure eights, and slide and glide in pairs. Have fun.

3. Now the mood quickly changes once more. The sun peeks out from behind a cloud. The ice begins to melt slowly and turn to slush. Uggh! What a mess! As the sun gets warmer, the ice melts completely. Walk on this slush in bare feet. How does this feel? How do *you* feel?

4. The mood quickly changes once again. Darkness closes in. (To simulate the mood, someone can turn off the lights.) Trees appear from seedlings in the ground and begin to sprout. Become your favorite animal or bird (or perhaps one that you think best expresses your personality). Relate to and become part of your new surroundings and habitat, be it a cave, a stream, a tree, whatever. *Ask yourself:* What am I? How do I feel? What can I do? Talk to your animal neighbor. Try to see the neighbor animal through the eyes of the animal or bird you have become. Think about the *specific* kind of animal or bird you are becoming. For example, perhaps you have become a frog, hopping around. But what kind of frog? A pop-eyed bullfrog who likes lakes and ponds? A tree frog? A warty American toad? And what about your sound? Try to capture the creature's movements, gestures, and facial expressions.

5. Now the animals go to sleep. Keep your eyes closed. Wake up as yourself. *Very* slowly, in exaggerated slow motion, feel yourself lift up and float into space. Leave behind the familiar sights and sounds of planet Earth as you begin your fantasy trip through time and space. What do you feel as you lift yourself up into another world? Can you describe the sensa-

Water-Woods-Window: But what kind of frog?

(Photo by Terry Buchalter)

tion to yourself? You wind up on the moon and float on the moonscape wearing your heavy astronaut shoes. Investigate carefully your newly created environment. Players may wish to work with others in smaller subgroups or scouting parties— exploring caves, volcanoes, rocks, and other environmental objects. Some of the players may wish to *become* the objects (in pairs or trios) found on the moon while others explore those objects.

6. After a few concentrated minutes of exploration, players come upon a large, mysterious, wonderful window in front of them. Crawl through it, and imagine the kind of world you would like to see and inhabit. Who and what live in this world? *Show* what kind of world it would be through your movements, the objects you handle, and the imaginary monsters, moon-people, or magical characters you encounter. This period of exploration should be done in *complete* silence. However, from time to time, players may wish to speak in gib-

Water-Woods-Window: Exploring on the moon . . . people and plants.
(*Photo by Leonard Lewis*)

berish, which is the repetition of nonsense syllables like *"Ooga salona forambi?"* for "How are you?" In gibberish, you can express and communicate emotions such as fear, anger, and surprise through the inflection of your voice and accompanying free-flowing gestures.

7. After a few more moments, walk to the edge of the moon's surface, and—that's right—fall off. Float down slowly through space, splashing down again into the pool where you started your journey.

8. Then all become, in mind and movement, little minnows who slither past one another in complete silence with their eyes closed, searching for the source of a stream in the center of the room. Find the center of your feelings—your own body tempo—as you let your imagination wander freely. Open your eyes, and experience others in the room as if for the first time. See if you are able to notice something new about them. Hold hands, and gently squeeze them.

9. Share your feelings about the fantasy trip with the rest of the group. How did it feel to let go, open up, and take a chance with your own creativity? When discussing your experiences, everyone's feelings—they will vary—should be respected.

Many players have commented on the dreamlike quality of the exercise, the unrelated and quickly changing environments—from forest to moon, and the actions that seem out of place. The dream effect is carried further in the poetry that players write after the experience.

EXPRESS WITH POETRY

You may wish to write "gut" reactions to the fantasy trip in poetry or to do a drawing. The window was the magic opening to whatever you wanted on the other side and, more importantly, an opening to your own insides—your imagination. Some poetic reactions to the magic window in workshops with young people and college students include the following:

> The window opened up into a big room
> Which was filled with ice cream
> It began to melt and fill the entire room.
> I found myself swimming and
> Eating my way out of the mess.
> ANNA EDGEHILL

> I knew it had to be a better place,
> A better world for every race.
> To live together in harmony
> To spread their leaves in ways so free.
> DENISE WRIGHT

> Mellow feelings,
> Gliding, floating,
> A one world—my own
> Quietness within
> Hustle bustle outside
> My own world—my own
> People around
> Part of the scene
> But do not penetrate
> My world—my own.
> SHELLEY TENZER

MOVING ON

MOVE TO MOODS AND COLORS

1. Everyone moves around the room in complete silence, alternating body rhythms—fast, slow, weak, strong, light, heavy.

2. *Shape* the flow of your motion by sculpting your body in rising and sinking movements, twisting and turning, advancing and retreating. Be aware of your shifts in posture. Trust your own body cues; explore the feelings hidden in the universe of your body.

3. Now move to colors suggested by the leader or different members of the group. Does red, for example, make you feel like moving fast or slow? Open or closed, happy or sad? Does it make you feel lonely, crazy, sunny, or what? Does yellow feel like a burst of sunshine, lazy dew, or what? Show us with your body.

Add other colors:

_____   _____

_____   _____

_____   _____

4. Now designate a leader to call out different words that are usually charged with emotion, such as

strong	food
love	(the name of your school)
America	hate
poverty	sun

Allow yourself to respond immediately. Feel the *essence* of the words without thinking about them too much. Thinking might edit your true muscular responses. Quickly *express* the words in *physical terms* with your body, and then *project* these feelings by magnifying the original impulse.

5. You may wish to combine with other players to enact spontaneously the essence of a word. This means simply joining another player's space and connecting some part of your bodies to evoke the feeling of the word. Emotional responses are "catching," and in no time at all, each player will absorb the contributions of others as if through osmosis.

Add your own words:

_____	_____
_____	_____
_____	_____

MOVING TO MUSIC

1. If music is used, it should be varied so that the players alternately move lazily (perhaps to "Lazy Day" by Spanky and His Gang) or sadly (perhaps to "Windows of the World") or happily to "Good Morning, Sunshine."

2. Make a "friendship train" (bodies connecting as ships and/or trains) that moves along snappily.

3. You can alternate moving and walking in super-fast time or in very slow motion. Use large expansive movements and smaller closed movements. Do not hesitate to adopt dance exercises, straddles, leg extensions; flexing and reaching in a creative context. Reach up toward the ceiling, beyond the ceiling to the sky, to the moon. Now come back to earth; drop from your waist, and reach for the ground. Your arms are drills; dig into the ground, and shake off the dirt. Vary size, shape, and intensity of the movements whenever possible. For example, move to the feeling of a great big, red neon sign, or capture the essence of tiny movements cut from crystal glass. Such images help the players to project their own movements creatively.

MOVE THROUGH OBSTACLES

Drama is perhaps the most dynamic of all the arts. It deals with conflict, danger, suspense. Everyone enjoys enacting situations and scenes in which we overcome obstacles, face danger, confront adverse natural conditions, and escape the perils of unforeseen circumstances. If it is fun to become another person, animal, or object, think how much more exciting it is when those creations find themselves in difficult situations.

1. Move around as yourself on different surfaces. Walk and run on grass, hot sand, slippery ice, gluey pavement; move *through* thick molasses, marshmallow, or mud—first wearing your slippers, then tennis shoes, army boots, and so forth.

2. Be yourself breaking out of a jelly glass; explore the sides with your whole body, and then try to escape. Be yourself trying to escape from a giant octopus (perhaps other players) engulfing you. Try moving around as a rubber ball through different obstacles.

3. Move through the crosscurrents of the ocean, adding overpowering weather conditions such as sleet, fog, or hail.

4. Become a character, animal, or object moving through adverse environmental conditions. How does it feel to be a chicken breaking out of its shell? A fly trying to extricate itself from flypaper? A butterfly caught in a spiderweb? A fish gasping for its last ounce of air? A tire being hit by a piece of glass, then slowly deflating? How does it feel to be a kite caught in the middle of an electric storm?

5. Become a floppy Raggedy Ann or Andy doll or a stiff wooden soldier moving through obstacles and then recovering from them—thus experiencing the alternate sensations of tension and relaxation. When moving as puppets, your partner can manipulate the strings from the center of your head to the center of your balance—the stomach. As a rag doll, stretch as tall as you can, all the way up to the sky, with feet squarely balanced, imagining that sawdust is trickling out of your body; and then

- Dangle your head all around.
- Swing your arms to and fro.
- Collapse loosely from your waist.
- Relax your arms, hands, and fingers.
- Breathe deeply.
- Straighten up slowly.
- Repeat several times.

Whether you move as a butterfly, an eel or a seal, a tadpole, an arrow, a guppy or a puppy, a spider, a snowflake or a raindrop suspended in midair, think of an environment or habitat for your character, animal, or thing; and work it into the movement. Be aware of the sudden impulsive cue, and learn to incorporate it into your deepest feelings.

INTEGRATING ICEBREAKERS

BUNCH OF BALLOONS

This sequence is an example of how several icebreakers can be integrated around one common object—in this case, a balloon.

1. Everyone lies on the floor, breathing slowly and deeply. Exhale all the air from your lungs; then inhale deeply through your nose. Hold your breath. Exhale.

2. Try it again, this time concentrating on making your breath slower, smoother. Try to think of energy as a light source, so that when you exhale, light is flowing through your whole body; your brain, in effect, is descending into the middle of a glowing warm body.

3. Imagine that a small balloon is inside you, attached to your spine by a string that extends through the top of your head. Now breathe more deeply, imagining that someone is pulling that string through your head.

4. Rise up slowly, and float around like a balloon. You *are* a balloon. (As one high-school student remarked: "I *really* became a balloon. I felt light and floaty in the air. I was even able to imagine myself being inflated. Fantastic!")

5. Now a pin suddenly hits you. Fizzle out. Slowly transform back into yourself.

6. Suddenly a bunch of imaginary balloons are released from the ceiling. Every time you try to grab one, it moves beyond your reach.

7. Now imagine there are pins on different parts of your body. See how many balloons you can burst. Pop! Pop! There goes another one! The more you *really* concentrate on those pins and balloons, the more creative fun you will have. (Poor balloons, how would you like it if someone did that number on *you*?)

8. Now *become* a limp balloon. Someone is blowing *you* up in four or five exhalations. Think of all the wonderful colors you can become. Let's hear the sound of the balloons filling up!

9. Continue expanding until you feel yourself beginning to rise almost to the top of the room—higher and higher. Feel the winds gently blowing you through the air.

10. Now someone punctures you with an imaginary pin. Let's hear the sound of escaping air. You collapse to the floor.

11. Continue with some more, light breathing exercises. After all that movement, you deserve a break.

12. In a circle formation again, pass around an imaginary floating balloon. Then play a game of catch with the balloon, transforming it into a hot ball, a cold ball, a bowling ball. And while we're on it, you can always play some group sports such as Ping-Pong, tennis, basketball—in pantomime, of course. The leader can get in as a player or umpire. Play the games in slow motion, adding sounds if you like.

Discussion of feelings can take place *after* experiencing the exercises, which can be freely adapted to the interests, needs, and developmental stages of the particular group or class. For example, the group members can list the different moods they experienced and discuss them.

NAME GAMES

The ability to address a person by his or her first name creates a friendly atmosphere conducive to exchanging ideas and feelings. Learning and having fun with one another's names can contribute greatly to the early familiarization stages in improvisational drama.

SPACE-WRITING

1. With your eyes closed, write your name in space (large and small movements). Imagine that your fingers are a piece of chalk or a paintbrush.

2. Add color to enlarge the name you are painting in the space around you.

3. Now use your whole arm as a brush, then your shoulders, your head, and finally your whole body. (Reactions include: "It was like erasing a blackboard with my body"; and "I felt like a sponge mopping up myself.")

4. Imagine your body as a giant hand molding clay. See how much space you can carve out for yourself, stretching and squeezing it as you feel necessary.

5. Work in pairs, writing *one* name in space. Accept the challenge of cooperation. Now, while your arms are relaxed, swing them one at a time in large circles.

6. Relax. You should now be in a state of relaxed energy. Yawn. Your face, neck, and vocal muscles should be completely relaxed. Ahhh! Your yawn will indicate how relaxed you are. Sitting in the circle, each player says his or her own name when it comes up. The pace quickens. Keep the names flowing around the circle. Now the players continue to pass names around at a steady pace, except that instead of saying your own name, say the name of any other player in the group. Go around the circle several times, passing around names.

MUTUAL INTERVIEW

As a form of introduction, telling about oneself can often be monotonous or even boring. In this exercise, energy is focused, because your partner must tell all about you!

1. In pairs seated in a circle, designate one player No. 1 and the other, No. 2.

2. For about three or four minutes, No. 1 interviews No. 2. (No notes, please!) Find out all you can about the other person's hobbies, favorite food, place of birth, favorite and least favorite plays and movies, and so forth and so on. You need not confine the interview to factual information, although there should be a certain amount of this. You can share a fantasy, mutual concerns, or whatever.

3. For three or four minutes, No. 2 then interviews No. 1.

4. Going around the circle in the large group, the players tell about their partners, each one starting off: "I'd like you to meet my friend, _____." Other players can ask questions as well.

5. If you find, when going around the circle awhile, that players need to refresh their memories about each other, simply have the remaining players reinterview the highlights for a minute or so.

CONCENTRATION GAME
1. Circle formation.
2. The first player chants and claps using his or her own name, then adds the name of anyone else in the circle. For example:

> John–ny, John–ny (two claps)
> Mar–y, Mar–y (also two claps or beats)

Then Mary starts with her name and adds another name:

> Mar–y, Mar–y
> Da–vid, Da–vid

The game continues with everyone getting a chance to say his or her name and to add someone's from the group. When the energy is high, the chanting and clapping can evolve into a beautifully confluent "jam session" with all kinds of rhythmical variations. As a variation, players can experiment with the feel of the names' sounds, such as "Mary, airy, Doug, dug, dlup, mud, and so on. These sounds, once they are transformed, can be utilized to realize the players' own vocal capabilities, which can later be used as sound effects.

THE TRIP
This is a delightful pantomime game, also known as "My Grandmother Is Going on a Trip."

1. The first player pantomimes making a trunk, box, or suitcase and puts something into it that he or she would need to make a trip, and that begins with the first letter of his or her name—for example, *Milt's magazine.*
2. The box is passed along to the next player, who first does something with Milt's magazine (let's say, reads it a bit), then puts it back into the box and puts in something beginning with the first letter of her first name (*Dina's drapes*).

The Trip: "I'm taking Stephanie's slippers . . ."
(Photo by Terry Buchalter)

3. The trunk is then passed around the circle, with each player saying all the preceding names in order and relating to all the other objects.

You will sense a story developing, with all the hilarious objects going into the box—Robert's rainwear, Stephanie's slippers, Ilya's ice cubes (melting!), Carla's cake, Shelly's snake tickling Kenny's kangaroo, and so forth. The group members may wish to draw pictures or write a story about their trip, as one class did about a "swinging" granny's visit to Jamaica.

MAKE UP A SKIT

After "The Trip" is played, each subgroup can make up a short skit (about five minutes or less) based on the objects mentioned. For example, Charlie's chipmunks, Irene's insect repellent, and the rest of the objects' names could, in this case, touch off a skit about a camping trip. Avoid taking *too* much time to plan the skit; ten minutes is sufficient.

MAKE UP YOUR OWN NAME GAME

A number of action songs can be adapted that involve pantomime, such as

You can't get to heaven on Larry's head
Because Larry's head is full of lead (or bread);
(pantomime the object)
Oh I ain't gonna grieve my Lord, no more!

Substitute other parts of the body; for example,

Because Larry's hand is full of sand.
(pantomime the object)

NAME GAME VARIATIONS

1. Act out your name for others. For example, for *Milton*, make a mill with your arms, and lift a ton of weights.

2. Take any exercise in this first chapter, and combine it with a name game. For example, when playing "Say Hello," put on name tags, but leave off the first letter of your first name. (Players will have fun guessing one another's names while breaking the ice.) Thus, *oy* could be *Roy* or *Joy; ilt* is *Milt; an* could be *Fran* or maybe *Stan*.

3. Whenever possible, write poetry after an exercise. One player, Denise Wright, wrote this poem after playing "Say Hello," wearing a name tag minus the first letter of her name:

You start by dropping the first letter of your name
Tag yourself and you've completed one step in the game,
Now move around the floor to the drum's staccato beat
And when it stops, "Say Hello" to the first person you
*   meet*
Sometimes you "Say Hello" with your head, shoulder, or
*   knee*
For, these are all different ways of saying "You are you
*   and I am me"*
And when it's all over, you've found that you've made
*   some brand new friends*
Who may not be around forever, but at least 'til the sum-
*   mer ends!*

Add your own name game:

_____

_____

_____

Whatever the season, have creative fun breaking the ice, and remember not to break the Icebreaker's Law:

Nothing is impossible for the person who does not have to do it!

SAMPLE SEQUENCES

In a forty-minute period, icebreakers should offer variety such as active/passive, and sitting/standing/moving. They should contain a mixture of movement and name games. Within any sequence, it is more fun for exercises to be progressively more challenging to the players.

JUNIOR HIGH

Say Hello
The Trip
Move to Moods and Colors
Stylized Tag

Magic Mover
Water-Woods-Window
Space-Writing
Bunch of Balloons

HIGH SCHOOL AND COLLEGE

Say Hello
Move to Moods and Colors
Magic Mover
Bunch of Balloons

Water-Woods-Window
Magic Mover
The Trip
Stylized Tag

PLAYER'S DIARY

1. How many ways did you say hello? How many different ways can you say good-bye?

2. What were your favorite ways of moving?

3. How did you feel moving through various obstacles? Which obstacles were more challenging than others?

4. What differences did you notice moving through the various environments of "Fantasy Trip"? What similarities?

5. What were your favorite name game exercises? Why?

Add your own questions, thoughts, and observations.

First darkness,
then the wind coming from the unknown
I moved at another's command
Led through space and many sensations
I found new lights in old stars
And a new light in me: trust!

Larry Guastella

THE POETRY OF TRUST 2

Often the most reliable sources of experience are the natural resources that lie within us—our feelings. In trust exercises, players work together to reach out and touch one another with the whole self. These nonverbal exercises are very important in group improvisation because they bring players closer together. Words, as we have seen, often mask true feelings, but through touch and the other senses, we can express and communicate the emotions we really feel.

BASIC TRUST EXERCISES

When done correctly, these exercises are perfectly safe. For the greatest enjoyment, they *must* be done in all seriousness. It is also very important that all the exercises be done in *com-*

plete silence (except for a leader's instructions), so that the players can reach deeper into themselves within the security of the group.

> Brief *discussions of feelings can take place* after experiencing the exercises. It is recommended that trust exercises follow several sessions of creative movement and name games, so that players will already have shared icebreakers, thus coming to know one another a little better and feeling more comfortable together.

LIFTING

1. The group is randomly divided into smaller subgroups of seven or eight players each (see *Forming Subgroups*, Appendix A).

2. In each group, one player volunteers to lie face up on the floor.

3. The rest of the people in the group put their hands under the player, and on signal from the leader (all others refrain from talking!), they lift the player first to shoulder height and then above their heads. Make sure the lifting is gentle and that *all* parts of the body (especially the head) are supported. In a soft voice, the exercise leader can use imagery to complement the mood of the lift. Here are three such examples: "You are King Tut being lifted from your tomb, higher and higher"; or "You are a light balloon, drifting with a warm air current"; "You are gently lifted on the soft wing of an eagle, carried off into the clouds." The person being lifted keeps his or her arms crossed against the chest and eyes closed throughout the exercise.

4. The player is gently swayed back and forth a few times.

5. The group lowers the player *slowly* and *gently* to the floor. Make sure hands are placed under the player's head as it is lowered. A good feeling of "support me" becomes evident in this exercise. One player described the experience as follows: "Picking people up, I felt like a tower of strength. I gently held each person's neck and head. I tried so hard to convey through touch that they need have no fear."

No one should be forced to participate if he or she does not wish to do so. Any reluctant players can give you their

Lifting: Every side of the body is supported.

(*Photos by Harout Merigan*)

reasons privately if they wish. Some students, on the other hand, may want to share their reasons. For example, one nursing student told her group she thought she was too fat. They told her that she need not worry; that they were, in fact, lifting some of the very big boys. She finally did participate, and the group seemed particularly sensitive toward her feelings.

A Note on Imagery. The use of imagery in the lifting greatly enhances relaxation. Players should have opportunities to compose such imagery. Here is an extended sample:

> *You are a leaf—ever so light. . . . on the count of 3, the soft southern winds will lift you ever so gently . . . 1–2–3—the lovely leaf up–up–up—ever higher . . . 1–2–3—gently swaying in the breeze, and now you are floating down . . . 1–2–3—you are so light—down you float . . . 1–2–3—you have landed—now rest, lovely leaf. . . .*

THE POETRY OF TRUST

It is always a good idea for the participants to write poetry after experiencing the lifting exercises. Some excerpts from college and high-school students:

> *Eyes closed, "Relax," they say*
> *And sixteen hands say, "Trust me."*
> *What a beautiful feeling to float*
> *With the warmth and comfort of*
> > *eight friends,*
> > *sixteen hands,*
> > *trusting!*
>
> SHELLEY TENZER

Up! A sense of timeless movement, the sheer
Delight of not knowing
Where you are . . .

The world drifted away,
I was weightless,
Floating on a sea of
Friendly hands . . .

ARLENE KOHN

In discussions following all trust exercises, focus attention on awareness: What are you experiencing *now?* What do you *feel* physically and emotionally?

BLIND WALK

1. The group is divided into pairs.

2. Each pair takes turns leading a partner, whose eyes are closed, around the room (or outside the room), exploring different spatial levels and tactile sensations.

3. The walk can take from a few minutes up to ten minutes. Explore going up and down stairs, down hallways, up and down escalators, etc.

We think this simple but highly effective exercise especially ignites a spark for creative writing, as the following student poems reveal:

The contoured chairs
The wind and breeze
That don't lead out
The uncertainty I feel
Demands I shout
But I don't . . .
I trust my "eyes"
I see my own skies
RAY SMITH

As darkness took my hand and led the way
I hedged and stopped and felt a sway
The hands and boards that touched my head
Gave rise to thoughts I could be dead
My feet were leaded down with weight
I knew my life was in the hands of my mate
DENISE WRIGHT

A fourth grader wrote:

I felt I needed him
And he needed me
Because none of us could see.
SEAN ROBERTS

Blind Walk
(*Photo by Harout Merigan*)

Discussions concerning the role of sight in our lives—on the different ways we can see without our eyes, the feeling of traveling through open and constricted spaces, how sound works as a guide, sharing experience about blind people—are especially fruitful and insightful after playing this game. One variation is to write the poetry or part of it with eyes closed, and another idea is for the blind-walk partners to read their poetry to each other. One player wrote the following poem directly after experiencing the exercise:

BLIND WALK
Grandpa, I wish others saw me the way you do.
You think I'm beautiful and your large hands
Tell me no lies.

As your strong, gentle arms and fingers gently
   Rock my shaking, frightened body
You see me as someone special—and others call you
   blind.

ELAINE WAGENSBERG

CIRCLE OF TRUST

1. The group makes about five or six smaller circles, with the players standing shoulder to shoulder and with feet close together.

2. A player volunteers to start and steps into the middle of the circle, closes his or her eyes, and falls backward.

3. The rest of the group catches the player and gently places him or her upright. The player in the center should relax every muscle. Some women in a group may be fearful that they will be pushed from the chest, so the leader should be sensitive in explaining to players to be careful about this aspect.

PANTOMIME PUPPETS

1. All the group members walk around the room and, on cue of the leader, transform themselves into puppets and continue to walk around the room.

Circle of Trust: The rest of the group catches the player and gently places him or her upright.
(*Photo by Jonathan Ishie*)

2. Periodically, go into a "freeze" position, relax, and isolate part of your puppet body. Imagine you have strings connected to these different parts as the leader calls out:

Move your fingers
Shake your neck
Lift your head
Drop your arms
Wiggle your toes

Add your own:

_____

_____

_____

3. Players are randomly divided into pairs. One player is the puppet; the other is the puppeteer.

4. All the puppets make one large circle and sing and clap to the song "Ponchinello":

Look, who's coming
Ponchinello, Ponchinello.
(One Ponchinello puppet is chosen.)

Look who's coming,
Ponchinello in the shoe.
(Ponchinello does some free rhythmic motion.)

Oh, what can you do,
Ponchinello, Ponchinello?
What can you do,
Ponchinello in the shoe?
(Others imitate Ponchinello.)

We can do it, too,
Ponchinello, Ponchinello
We can do it too,
Ponchinello in the shoe.
(New Ponchinello is chosen, and song repeats.)

5. The puppeteer controls the puppet's movements (see how many familiar things players can do, like brushing teeth,

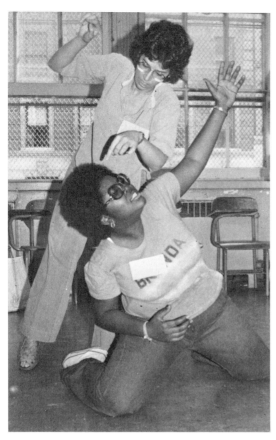

Pantomime Puppets: Imagine you have strings connected to different parts of your body.

(Photo by Leonard Lewis)

painting a wall, shining shoes, eating a candy bar, clapping hands), so that the puppet really becomes dependent on the puppeteer.

6. On signal of the leader, puppeteer leaves puppet alone, to collapse.

7. Repeat steps 5 and 6 with puppet and puppeteer reversing roles.

8. Players change slowly back into real people.

9. Discuss why trust is so important. Discuss differences between people and puppets and why trust is so important among people. How can people receive trust without controlling one another? Can the players, in pairs, create simple sketches where people help each other? For example:

- A newcomer to a strange city asking for directions.
- A young person helping an elderly person across the street.
- An elderly person helping a very young child across the street.
- Someone finding a stray kitten in an alley.

Add your own:

_____

_____

_____

BY YOURSELF
AND WITH OTHERS

PERSONAL COAT OF ARMS
A personal coat of arms is a way of looking at one's life up to now. To complete the coat of arms, answer the following questions by drawing a picture, symbol, or design that repre-

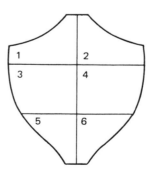

sents your answer in each area of the coat of arms. Do not use words except in space 6.

1. What do you regard as your greatest personal achievement to date?

2. What do you regard as your family's greatest achievement?

3. What is the one thing that other people can do to make you happy?

4. What do you regard as your own greatest personal failure to date?

5. What would you do if you had one year to live and were guaranteed success in whatever you attempted?

6. What three things would you most like to be said of you if you died today?*

Feel free—as Simon, Howe, and Kirschenbaum suggest in their excellent book—to substitute other values and questions:

1. What is a personal motto you live by?

2. What is something you are striving to become? Or to be?

3. What is something about which you would never budge?

Add your own:

4. _____

5. _____

6. _____

A Note. The drawings in your personal coat of arms can be simple, unintelligible to others, even incomplete—as long as you understand what they express. It is up to the players themselves whether or not they want to share the significance of their drawings. It is not easy to say exactly what you value.

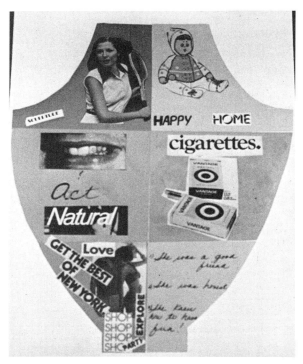

A personal coat of arms.
(*Photo by Terry Buchalter*)

Values are often private; they often change, and they often conflict. But this exercise helps the players at least to ask what they want in their lives and what they are doing to get what they want. If you wish to share your coat of arms, you can make a "gallery walk" or a "values museum" or post the drawings in the classroom.

EVERYONE'S A STAR!

This exercise provides a chance for the players to share a bit about themselves while having creative fun.

1. Everyone is instructed to draw a five- or six-pointed star with the following information big enough for another player to see.

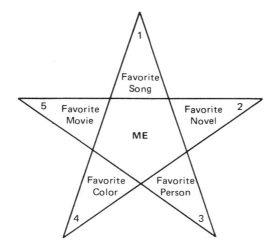

Other categories might include favorite poem, play, city, and so forth.

Add your own:

_____

_____

_____

2. Players pin their homemade stars on their own shirts or blouses.

3. Players walk around and introduce themselves to one another (as in "Say Hello," Chapter 1).

4. Periodically, the leader (or one of the players) yells "freeze!" and the rest of the players freeze. Then the leader calls out a category on the star. In pairs, the players act out for each other in pantomime the essence of the category. For example, if it's "favorite play," the player might imagine being in a chorus line doing some kicks.

5. After players have had opportunities to share and exchange their favorites, the entire group can make one gigantic star, exploding with energy. Here's how: Players start by touching their fingers to one another; they spin in various orbits closer together, make a sound chord in unison that slowly builds, and finish by breathing together, bursting into one big (controlled) shout (perhaps accompanied by the beat of a drum, hand claps, or turning on and off of the lights).

One player wrote the poem that opens the chapter after experiencing the exercise. Have fun figuring out your own variations of this and the other exercises.

On this note of trust, we conclude the chapter. The exercises included are especially effective as a warm-up in the beginning of the term and at the start of any particular drama session. So pick and choose, and have fun trusting yourself and others.

SAMPLE SEQUENCES

The following are three sample sessions incorporating exercises from the first two chapters:

Say Hello	Puppets
Magic Mover	Circle of Trust
Magic Mover	Water-Woods-Window
Pantomime Puppets	Blind Walk
The Trip	Bunch of Balloons
Magic Mover	Lifting

PLAYER'S DIARY

1. How did you feel doing the exercises? What did you learn? Did you trust yourself to take creative risks, to take a chance? Did you trust others? Why? Why not?

2. How did it feel to be "blind"?

3. Why is it important to be a good leader? How did it feel to be a leader?

4. Did you recognize objects with your eyes closed? Were you aware of what was going on around you?

5. How did it feel to fall backwards in the Circle of Trust? Did you feel safe? Did you trust others to catch you? Did you trust yourself to catch others?

6. Think about this: When is language really necessary? When a stranger asks another person the way to a certain place? When consoling a widow about the loss of her husband? When saying hello in different ways?

7. What does your name mean? If you don't know, how can you discover its derivation?

8. Talk about this: What is trust? How do we learn to trust ourselves and each other?

9. What is nonverbal communication? What are some examples?

10. Whom do you trust most? Why?

Add your own questions, thoughts, and observations.

SENSORY AWARENESS EXERCISES 3

Quick—what color is the shirt you're wearing? Can you describe the feel of the paper you're touching right now? Can you isolate all the sounds in the room where you're sitting? Have you really seized the opportunity to see into another person's eyes lately, to note all the intricacies of that person's face, to become aware of the marvelous structure of the human body? And what about the senses of taste and smell? Have you really used them to the fullest in your everyday life?

The following mind relaxers and concentration builders can help to finely resharpen and retune sensory awareness. We are multisensorial creatures. Most of our early learning about the world comes through sensory awareness. As children, we explored—through touch and movement—the mysteries of life with a fresh openness and vitality. Try as many exercises as time allows. They can be done almost anytime during a class or workshop period but are especially effective at the beginning of a session.

41

TOUCHING

"Keeping in touch" is one of the most overworked phrases in the English language; yet touch itself is one of the most neglected senses. So many of the emotions are expressed through touch that it is imperative for those involved in improvisation to have opportunities to experience the sensation of touch in a friendly, noncompetitive atmosphere. Touch provides almost instant awareness about another human being. Recall from your own childhood that one way of "seeing" was through touch. It was your earliest guide when, as a baby, you crawled along the floor or were held in your mother's arms. Touch is a powerful means of expression that can release so many truthful feelings. Only later does voice come to substitute for (or complement) this basic sensation. Touch, as a nonverbal form of communication, can open up a great deal of verbal expression.

SELF-AWARENESS

STREAM OF SAND
1. The entire group lies down on the floor. Everyone breathes deeply.

2. Imagine that you are stretched out on your back on the beach. It is very hot, but you are relaxed—very relaxed.

3. Imagine that a warm stream of sand is passing through your body, starting in your left toe, then coursing its way s-l-o-w-l-y from toe to toe, through your left foot, up your ankle and leg, through your kneecap, up the whole left side of your body, through your hair, and down the right side of your head and the rest of your body, ending in the right toe.

4. Take your time. There will be much to explore, as the skin is the largest organ of the body. Pause especially at the neck. Note if it is tense or relaxed. Feel the safety and security of the friendly floor against your back.

Concentration is the key: The key to real relaxation is the ability to concentrate on one sensation at a time. Take your time. Ask yourself, what am I doing now, and how does it make me feel? What am I learning about myself—how do I feel about myself now?

ADD SOME WATER

1. Now reach into an imaginary bucket of water right next to you. Make that bucket *real* by picturing it clearly in your mind. What does it look like?

2. Wet your hands in the "bucket," and, starting with your hair and *keeping your eyes closed,* explore your own body in a process of self-touch. Discover the sensations of your body as you explore it with your hands. Ask yourself what parts feel hardest, smoothest, softest, roughest?

3. Sense your relationship to the floor. How does your body feel against it? Comfortable? Uncomfortable? What is the feeling?

4. Note the similarities of bony cartilage and the fleshy parts of your ears, nose, and the hollows under your cheekbones. Try to see the relationships between one part of the body and the next.

5. How do your jewelry and clothing feel in relation to your skin?

6. Vary the pressure of touch, and perceive the variations from rigid bone to softer cartilage.

7. Contract and relax different parts of your limbs. Breathe . . . let all the good sunshine pour through your veins.

After experiencing this exercise, one student remarked:

I've never been aware of my body as part of me. I wash my body, I brush my teeth, I lotion my legs; but I never truly was aware of these things. It was just a habit. But touching my body in class, I realized how strong my legs were, how smooth my skin was and how rough in other parts. I became proud of my body: a sort of self-actualization. It's amazing how this realization took place on a dusty floor in school.

GROUP AWARENESS

THE CRAWL

1. Remain in a lying position with your eyes closed. Start to crawl slowly along the floor. (Imagine that you are a worm or other crawly thing.)

2. At the appropriate signal (drum, clap of hands, etc.), reach out and touch the person next to you. Concentrate on the head, hair, face, neck, arms, hands, and fingers of the person you touch. (In the early growth process, touch precedes visual recognition: It is the first contact we have with things and people.) Think to yourself: How does it feel to touch in the dark?

3. Once in a while, whoever is conducting this exercise should ask the players to open their eyes, so they may experience the joy of recognizing the person they are with. Ask yourself: How do I feel? What am I experiencing *now?*

4. Upon opening your eyes, look into the eyes of the other person. (Our eyes have been called the first medium of expression, because they locate people and things. They have also been called the "window of the soul," because they reveal so many of our true feelings. Pause to think of the many encounters in daily life that begin with eye contact.)

5. Close your eyes again, and continue to crawl on the floor. On signal from the leader, reach out and touch your new neighbor. Background music, such as "The First Time Ever I Saw Your Face," may be added.

6. Write poetry—your feelings—about this experience with touch. What emotions were released? How much could you "see" with your hands?

A Note About the Exercise: Normally, we feel embarrassed when we have to touch another person outside of shaking hands. Many playing this touch game have realized how newcomers to a school or neighborhood must feel, as strangers. One player noted: "Once contact was made, however, I felt relieved, knowing it wasn't as bad as I thought it would be, and came to the realization that perhaps other persons felt the same way." Another player remarked: "When I felt someone touching my hands, I got a feeling of being

The Crawl: Reach out and touch the person next to you.
(*Photo by Harout Merigan*)

wanted." Hopefully, these touching exercises will enable the players to shed feelings of self-consciousness (shame of the body) and will instill feelings of self-confidence (pride in the body as a beautiful instrument of expression and creation).

TOUCH BOX

1. The group prepares a "touch box" or bag containing a wide variety of surfaces and materials, such as sandpaper, glass, fur, fabrics, leather, stones, something sticky, and so forth. *Add your own:*

_____

_____

_____

2. Try to describe in a few words the tactile sensations you experience handling each object while blindfolded or with eyes closed.

3. Associate and describe each sensation with its opposite surface or feeling—for example, something wet with something dry. The sandpaper felt rough, and the glass felt _____.

4. Discuss the different ways we can "see" with our hands and other parts of the body. Compare the size, weight, and shape of things touched.

Extending the Blind Walk: We can "see" with our hands.
(*Photo by Harout Merigan*)

TASTING AND SMELLING

Taste and smell, as Lewis and Streitfeld note in *Growth Games*, are usually de-emphasized in a culture that makes closeness of nearly any sort unwelcome.* Yet these senses are very important to the appreciation and understanding of the total sensory makeup of the individual.

* Howard R. Lewis and Harold S. Streitfeld, *Growth Games* (New York: Harcourt Brace Jovanovich, 1970), p. 50.

TASTE BOX

For this exercise, all foods used must be *harmless*.

1. Prepare a box or bag of objects that can be tasted. As with the touch box, many of these objects can be obtained from home, such as a tube of toothpaste, a jar of apple sauce, a lemon, a roasted marshmallow, some sharp cheddar cheese, raisins, a dill pickle.

2. Pass the *real* objects around, and have each player describe their taste while blindfolded.

3. Pass an *imaginary* object around, and describe its taste.

4. Ask yourself: What foods do I like to eat? What foods don't I like? What are some sweet foods I like and don't like? What are some sour foods I like and don't like?

The sense of taste is very important in the appreciation of the total sensory makeup of an individual...
(*Photo by Leonard Lewis*)

SENSORY AWARENESS EXERCISES

. . . as is the sense of smell.
(Photo by Alex Gersznowicz)

5. Can you isolate the tastes of sweetness and bitterness? The sensations of hot and cold? Discuss how tastes communicate things we like and don't like.

6. Move around the room the way a taste makes you feel. (For example, the taste of peanut butter makes me feel crunchy and together; the taste of vinegar makes me feel shivery and loose.)

PASS AROUND SMELLS

1. Make a list of smells that you like and don't like.

2. Collect objects brought from home in a "smell-me box" or jar. Examples include perfume, sugar, cinnamon, camphor balls, paint, room-freshener sprays.

3. Players are blindfolded or close their eyes tightly. Now smell the different objects brought in. Again, these should all be *safe* smells.

4. Identify a place with each object, such as baking powder with the kitchen; talcum powder with the bathroom; mothballs with a closet.

5. Certain foods have different personal associations for different people. For example, what does the smell of frying bacon suggest to you? Breakfast? Camping? A favorite restaurant?

6. Make a mental picture of an *imaginary* object, and describe its smell or odor. Really see the image—believe in it with all your energy. Connect an action with the object and the smell. For example, in your imagination:

- See a rose, feel it, pick it, and smell it. React naturally.
- See a garbage pail, take the top off, and smell it. React naturally.
- See some freshly baked cake, pick up a piece, and smell it. React naturally.

Add your own:

- See a fish market. (action–reaction)
- See a hot oven. (action–reaction)
- See an animal in a pet store. (action–reaction)

SMELLS OF THE DAY

Divide into subgroups, and act out short skits, observing and reacting to smells during one segment of the day or evening. For example:

WAKE UP IN THE MORNING
- Wake up and yawn.
- Go to the window, open up, and smell the air. Notice how you feel because of it.
- Go to the bathroom, see and smell the soap, and wash your hands and face.
- See and smell the toothpaste, and brush your teeth.
- See and smell your clothes, and dress.
- See and smell eggs, and eat them.

- See and smell dirty dishes, and wash them.
- See and smell garbage, and take it out.
- See and smell kitty litter, and change it.

After the group skits, the rest of the players can contribute comments and discuss how the skits could be improved. Replaying, using other times of day, takes place after a brief discussion.

HEARING

It has been estimated that most people operate at only a 25 percent level of efficiency when they are listening. Onstage, as in life, it is imperative that the creative actor—and person—sharply develop this sense.

REAL AND IMAGINARY SOUNDS

1. Listen carefully to, and make a list of, all the sounds you hear in the room. Classify the sounds into pleasant sounds, unpleasant sounds, loud sounds, soft sounds, familiar sounds, strange sounds, and so forth. Express how the sounds feel with different parts of your body, such as swinging your arm emphatically or limply. Use your whole body to show how sound feels.

2. Try the exercise again with your eyes closed. Listen carefully to the shutting of a door, the opening of a window, an airplane or insect buzzing. Note the differences in sound. Make believe you are in a dark room, looking for something you have lost. While you are in the "dark room," someone can play tape-recorded sounds that are interpreted by the rest of the group. For example, an alarm clock may conjure up the mental picture of someone drowsily rising for work, or of a fire chief sliding down a fire pole. Alternate listening to sounds with your eyes open for a minute and then with them closed. How did closing and opening your eyes alter the relationship of the sea of space seen around you? How did it affect your inner space?

3. Listen to imaginary sounds—the siren of an ambulance, a bird call, a clock ticking, a dog barking, a loud crash. Someone in the group can call out the sound, with the others reacting to it.

PASS AROUND SOUNDS

1. The group forms a circle.

2. Before passing around some sounds, use appropriate imagery to suggest the steady flow of sound—for example, a steady stream of water flowing around an inner tube, a circular wind tunnel conducting soft sounds around and around. The first player starts with one sound; this is carefully passed from player to player sitting in the circle. Pass around words, and give them vocal coloration. For example, say the word *soft* softly and *quick* quickly, *glue* with a sticky quality, *red*—however the player interprets it.

3. The second time around, the person on the right picks up the sound exactly and then transforms it into another sound.

SOUND COLLAGE

1. The group discusses a theme of particular interest—for example, neighborhood, politics, world affairs.

2. Each person chooses a word, phrase, or sound that evokes a feeling of the chosen theme. For example, for the neighborhood theme, words and sounds chosen could be *pollution, wow, taxicabs, swissssh!* and so on.

3. Form two rows—one sitting, the other standing directly behind.

4. A "conductor" volunteers to lead the players as in an orchestra.

5. Take turns pointing to one another (repeat sound, phrase, or word). Someone holds fingers to lips to indicate a softer or louder, shorter or stretched out sound.

6. Add in place movements that complement their sounds.

7. Add an accompanying gesture that relates to the sound chosen.

CREATING SKITS FROM SOUNDS

1. Each group (consisting of four or five players) thinks of about six sounds that when linked together will form the sequence of a story. For example: the sound of footsteps, the sound of a door opening preceded by several knocks, the sound of a creaky rocking chair, the sound of a book dropping, the sound of running on a floor, dialing of a phone, a scream.

2. These sounds are then tape-recorded or made on the spot while the rest of the players' eyes are closed.

3. Divide into four or five different subgroups, which then create and enact their version of the situation based on the sounds received. For example, based on the sounds of knocking, rocking, dialing of phone, and a scream, someone could be in a rocking chair reading a book when an intruder enters and frightens her. She is unable to complete her call for help.

4. Additional sounds that flesh out the story can be added.

5. The sounds and stories chosen for the skits should be simple, short, and *clear*, with a beginning (the conflict introduced), middle (conflict developed), and end (conflict resolved).

6. For evaluation, discuss what was happening. Was the action clear? What other sounds and movements may have been used?

7. The skits can then be replayed and reevaluated. Take turns leading discussion: Did the group use imagination, concentration, and teamwork? In what specific ways?

SEEING

Through the sense of sight, we observe and perceive the world around us, from the smallest ant crawling on the ground to towering buildings, birds flying in the sky, and the myriad shapes of nature at work. It is one thing to look and another to observe with clarity and understanding. Knowing how to look—seeing shapes and relationships and sensing connections—with concentration to details adds up to observation. The ability to see and respond keenly is essential to improvisational work. We all see things differently because we experience things differently. But whatever it is we see, it is important to develop a sense of trust in our own powers of vision and perception. To develop trust, you need self-confidence, which comes from being at one with yourself, believing in yourself—that you have an original contribution to make—and taking the time to use your natural creative potential to the fullest.

EYE EXPANSION
The human eyeball weighs one-quarter of an ounce and has a diameter of slightly less than one inch; yet it is capable of extraordinary vision. Give your eyes *super* X-ray vision by trying on some special glasses.

1. Focus your eyes on something in particular directly above you—something to your right. Be specific as to what you see—a crack in the wall, a cobweb on the ceiling, a marking on the blackboard. Now focus down on the floor; then to your left. Go slowly. Each time, try to stretch your eyes. Blink them a few times. Relax.

2. Repeat the exercise; but this time, pause after each focus, and add your TV-camera eyes. For example:

- *Long shot*—the object has not been completely isolated, but it is in focus.
- *Medium shot*—the shot is in sharper focus, good detail.
- *Close up*—the shot is magnified ten times. Sharpest detail, concentration excellent, hold. . . .
- *Pan* your camera eyes vertically and horizontally, and repeat the process.

PASS AROUND FACES
St. Jerome wrote: "The face is the mirror of the mind, and . . . without speaking, confesses the secrets of the heart." Do we really take the time to see into another person's eyes, to note all the hills and valleys of that person's face, to become aware of its marvelous structure and varied textures?

1. Circle formation. The first player starts with one face and makes a mask of it, then passes it around the circle, where it is copied exactly. Try to think of the masks as being made of rubber, so that the faces are really rubberized. (The sillier, the better!) This exercise, in addition to enhancing visual discrimi-

53

Make a mask of your face, and pass it on to someone else.
(*Photo by Claudia M. Caruana*)

nation, helps to break down inhibitions. One student, for example, remarked: "Some of the people who seemed the 'straightest' made the weirdest faces. The manner in which people 'let go' is really funny." No talking permitted, but a sound may accompany the facial expression.

2. The second and subsequent times around the circle, each player carefully picks up the mask he or she receives from the person on the right and transforms it into a different mask. When a player has made a mask, and a sound, the new player transforms *both* the mask and the sound.

Each player, therefore, has the chance to create something personal but must first concentrate on what his or her neighbor has made. Passing around and transformation exercises are excellent for developing group trust and give-and-take. People cannot help but be flattered when they are imitated, and this shores up self-confidence and good feelings.

3. When passing around faces, try to become aware of the different ways facial muscles combine to form expressions. How many different ways are there to smile, to frown, to laugh? How many different ways can one facially express anger, sorrow, fear, surprise, jealousy?

The face is capable of more than a thousand different forms of subtle expressions. In fact, the face is the greatest area of expression in the human body. Seventeen muscles are required for smiling, forty-three to frown. Consider one of Marcel Marceau's famous mimes called "The Mask Maker." Marcel depicts a number of facial masks showing a variety of expressions—effervescence, blandness, melancholy, chagrin—finally reaching one mask he cannot change, even if his life depends on it. And indeed it does, for he has created a mask of death. Try as he may—pulling on it, trying to tear it off—he cannot change it. The rest of his body expresses his fear and fury—he begins to tremble and shake—his arms and legs weaken—he loses all strength, staggers, and collapses to the floor. Death is the unremovable mask of life.

How many different ways can you twist and contort your face, stretching its twenty-four pairs of muscles? This is a good exercise to practice at home, using a mirror.

SENSORY WALK

Now that the senses have been isolated for closer work, you may wish to integrate them in one experience that can be shared by all the group members. Take a walk to a mutually agreed-upon place. For example, an elementary-school class might visit a farm, perhaps *seeing* certain animals for the first time, *touching* their soft fur, *listening* to all the sounds on the farm, *smelling* all the odors, perhaps *tasting* cow's milk or wonderful fruit jams. Another class might take a walk just outside school, *seeing* all the different neighborhood inhabitants—old people, people working and playing, lovers, angry people; *touching* textures and surfaces heretofore unnoticed; *smelling*, perhaps for the first time, odors peculiar to the neighborhood; *tasting* foods from nearby stores; *listening* to all the sounds one takes the time to hear—in short, becoming more aware of all the life around.

This awareness is even more intensified through improvising the things you saw, touched, heard, smelled, and tasted. Then, after recapturing this experience through doing, you can discuss what you were doing. You certainly will have a great deal to recount, whether you journey to a farm, the seashore, or city streets.

If you wish to enact a "Sensory Happening," different subgroups can be assigned to or can volunteer for each one of the senses and prepare appropriate activities. Then all the senses can be combined into one unified final event. For example, players can make a Sensory Mural, a creative concoction of pictures, photos, drawings, and poetry integrated with the live movement, mime, and music.

Body and sensory awareness exercises, whether used on-stage or in school, can never really be completed, of course, as they are a continuing part of the ongoing process of everyday life. These kinds of exercises, in which the human spirit is seen from many sides, are practiced in different forms of the Human Potential Movement. Much of the movement is predicated on the opening up of the senses to experience the joy of living and to sustain a more positive self-image in relationship to other people. Many more exercises devoted to sensory awareness appear in this book. We conclude this chapter with a fascinating game called *Polluter*.

POLLUTER

1. The players move around the room in scattered formation for a few minutes with their eyes closed.

2. The leader designates one player as the Polluter by tapping his or her shoulder.

3. Now all the players keep their eyes open and move around the room.

4. When the Polluter winks at one of the other players, that player must fall down about five seconds after the Polluter has passed. At any time, the players can guess who the Polluter is.

The game really works beautifully in establishing high-intensity eye contact. It is unfortunate that the game, in fact, is called *Polluter,* because it really brings people close together in such a lively and lovely way. It is as it says in the song "The Shadow of Your Smile" by Johnny Mandel and Paul Francis Webster: "Look into my eyes, my love, and see/All the wond'rous things you are to me. . . ."

There are several ways in which the exercises in this chapter can be combined into exciting creative sequences. The arrangements depend on the size of the group, how much time is available, and the age level and developmental needs and interests of the group. Whenever possible, the teacher and the participants are urged to make their own variations of exercises and sequences. It is always important, however, to allow for a variety of lying down, sitting, standing, and moving levels as well as differences in activity and passivity.

SEQUENCE 1
- Stream of Sand, Add Some Water, and The Crawl—lying down.
- Touch Box and Pass Around Sounds—sitting.
- Creating Skits from Sounds—sitting and standing.

SEQUENCE 2
- Pass Around Faces—sitting.
- Stream of Sand—lying down.
- The Crawl—lying down and moving on the floor.
- Creating skits based upon facial movements.

SEQUENCE 3
- Pass Around Faces—sitting.
- Eye Expansion—sitting and standing.
- Taste Box and Pass Around Smells—sitting.
- Creating skits based upon sensory awareness.

PLAYER'S DIARY

1. What color is your hair? Your eyes? The clothing you are wearing today?

2. What is the design and feel of fabric of the clothes you are wearing right now?

3. Can you describe the design and feeling of your body?

4. What is so special about your nose? How are taste and smell related? What items smell the same to you? Can you describe three foods which taste differently?

5. Why is it so important to listen?

6. Can you make a list of all the sounds you listened to today?

7. How can you tell the difference between the different shapes and sounds in your room? Outside your room in one particular place?

8. What does being aware mean to you?

9. What role does stillness play in awareness? What role does concentration play in awareness?

10. How can you become even more aware of yourself and others? List two or three *specific* ways.

Add your own questions, thoughts, and observations.

MAKING MIRRORS AND MACHINES 4

Mirroring is one of the best exercises for developing concentration. Making machines enables players to transform concentrated energy into exciting creative efforts.

When combined with sensory work or meditation, the two exercises provide a wonderful 1–2–3 warm-up activity (found at the end of this chapter).

MIRROR IMAGES

Human mirror-making is as old as the dawn of history, when people gazed in wonder upon their reflections in pools of water. They looked into the still waters, not out of vanity, but to view their fate. For example, if the image was distorted by ripples, it was taken as a portent of evil. Primitive men and women imagined that the picture they saw was not the reflection of a personal image but of the very soul. They thought the soul could detach itself and have an independent existence. If the mirror were broken, the soul too could be shattered.

Making human mirrors helps us to become more aware of and sensitive to our fellow human beings. The exercise promotes a heightened sense of timing and working closely together in pairs and in groups. When people take their time to make the exercise work, a beautiful rhythm becomes evident along with a sense of genuine, harmonious contact and cooperation.

HOW TO MAKE MIRRORS

As a motivation or lead-in to the exercise, you may wish to play an appropriate song, such as the tender "Let Me Be Your Mirror" (Hal David and Michel Legrand).

Discuss what you see when you look into a mirror and what you think reflections are. What, in addition to physical images, can be reflected? Discussion can center around the reflection of moods, states of mind, and expressions.

1. Work with a partner. Someone be Player 1, the other, Player 2. Sit or squat close together, looking into each other's eyes as if for the first time. Explore each other's eyes, and "lock in" for ten seconds or so.

2. Player 1 initiates a slow movement of his or her facial features while Player 2 imitates it exactly. Stretch your face into many expressions. After a while, Player 2 initiates the motions while Player 1 imitates them exactly. We all become a little flattered when other people imitate what we do, and a bit of friendly flattery never hurt the ego.

3. Observe specific parts of the face while taking turns being the initiator and the reflector. For example, observe the brows in motion. Do they show attention, indifference, displeasure, worry, or what? What expressions does the mouth convey in different combinations of mouth corner and lip positions? What emotions are expressed when the lips are opened up wide (surprise and awe)? When slightly opened, with mouth corners down (disgust)? When the corners are

Look into each other's eyes . . . go slow . . . and keep eye contact.
(*Photo by Tom Fridy*)

even and the lips closed (attention)? When slightly opened (anticipation or numbness)? Check closely the other combinations of expression, as when the brows are down, showing anger. Someone can call out various emotions, and the players will mirror each other's interpretation of the emotional state.

anger	fright
surprise	happiness
worry	sadness

Add your own:

_____   _____

_____   _____

_____   _____

4. Commence the *slow* movement of your arms, hands, and upper body as if under water, using the immediate space around you. First, Player 2 is the mirror and must reflect precisely all of Player 1's expression and movement. Take turns initiating simple activity pantomime, such as eating peanut butter, peeling an orange and eating it, molding an imaginary object from clay. With your hands, say "hello," "good-bye," "yes," "no," "perhaps." With your face, say "I'm feeling great," "lousy," "blah," or "I'm sick," "sleepy," "starry-eyed." Put on clothing; play a sport. Do something fantastic or familiar. (Remarked one player: "I didn't know until this workshop that I open my mouth when I put on mascara. Talk about self-awareness!")

5. Reverse roles. Take your time. Observe the subtleties of facial and body movements together—for example, hand-to-neck movements that may indicate defensiveness, or hand-rubbing-nose movements that may indicate ambivalence about something.

6. Now open your eyes as widely as possible, and inhale deeply. Squeeze your eyes as tightly as possible, and exhale forcibly.

Mirroring in pairs, standing up and using the whole body.
(*Photo by Mary Alfieri*)

DEVELOPMENT

1. Continue mirroring in pairs, standing up and using the whole body.

2. Add a *soft* sound that evolves from the movement.

3. At the sound of a drum (or clap of hands), slide over and continue to play mirror with the person nearest you.

4. The exercise leader can call different combinations of mirrors—working in pairs, threes, fives.

5. Eventually, if the give-and-take is sharp enough, one large, pulsating group mirror will emerge, with everyone participating enthusiastically!

For improvisational drama, a group mirror, when working well, is a great indicator that individual souls are making contact and communicating with one another. If group mirrors do not work at first, try them again at a later time. The results will be surprising.

MOVING MIRRORS

These are fun to do, adding soft sounds whenever appropriate. Perhaps you recall, from the movie *Duck Soup,* the delightful

Moving Mirrors: Add soft sounds whenever appropriate.
(*Photo by Rhoda Cohen*)

MAKING MIRRORS AND MACHINES

scene of Groucho Marx and his brother Harpo both dressed in long nightgowns, standing in front of a hotel-room mirror, delightfully mimicking each other—kicking one foot in the air, doing the Charleston, dropping their hats, stepping out of the mirror, and so forth.

Moving mirrors spark ensemble interaction and are good preparation for actors playing off each other in improvisational scenes. Players can make mirrors as they move from one side of the room to the other; one side is controlled by fast and soft sounds, the other by slow and loud sounds with accompanying movement. Imagine that your head is a TV camera; go in for close-ups, long shots, panning and trucking shots. Be playful and have fun.

USES

IN THE CLASSROOM

It should be noted that mirroring can be tied in with a variety of school subjects. In an elementary-school classroom, a group of students studying science played mirroring, utilizing the fact that Venus, our closest planet, is about the same size as Earth and is indeed known as our twin sister. In science, mirroring can help illuminate the concept of cloning, crystal formation (right- and left-handed versions), and molecular structure. You can make a musical mirror to "Skip to My Lou," as did teacher Ruth Whitted, with the following changes:

Look at your partner, two by two
Look at your partner, two by two
Do what your partners do, do, do
This is a facial mirror.

Now add gestures, two by two
Now add gestures, two by two
Do what your partners do, do, do
Gestures within a mirror.

IN THE THEATER

Mirroring can also be very effective in theater presentations. Human mirrors have held a prominent place in the performing arts through the ages. A striking example is the "Mirror Dance" from the ballet *La Ventana* by the nineteenth-century Danish choreographer, August Bournonville. In this country, human mirrors were first popularized by Viola Spolin.* In one production presented by the Haitian Kovidor Group, a distorted mirror technique was used to present two sides of a character's personality. Rea Jacobs, after experiencing the mirror game improvisationally, wrote an interesting play for her high school students in which a teenager named Michael is mysteriously confronted by his mirror image. Michael, through the help of his alter-ego mirror, learns to reconcile his fantasies with the reality around him and grows more capable of living with himself.

DISCUSSION AND EVALUATION

A discussion can ensue about how it felt to make mirrors and what the students learned from one another. An interesting discussion about cultural nonverbal expression of values may take place. For instance, the lack of direct eye contact between children and adults, and between subordinates and those in authority, is a sign of respect within the Puerto Rican community. Some students recalled being reprimanded when they were children for not looking their teachers squarely in the face.

Whenever possible, the use of videotape can facilitate the process of peers learning from one another. Questions can include the following: Did you feel a closeness to and an empathy with your partner? What were you saying to your partner? What do you think and feel your partner was saying to you? Were you able to play mirroring more effectively with certain players and not as well with others? Why? Why not?

Mirror images help us to see ourselves in others. Players should share what they get out of each session. One player remarked: "Mirroring gave me perspective; we never really see ourselves as others do." Commented another: "She's hysterical. Look at her doing everything I do. I can really maneuver

* Viola Spolin, *Improvisation for the Theater* (Evanston: Northwestern University Press, 1963), p. 60.

her around. I open my mouth, and she opens hers. I stick out my tongue, and she sticks hers out right back at me. Ha! I got her—she can't wink. Hey world, she can't wink! She sure looks funny imitating me. I guess so do I."

THEMES FOR MIRRORING
1. Mirrors from famous stories, such as *Snow White*
2. Family roles (fathers, mothers, children, grandparents)
3. Activities during different parts of the day
4. Different sports activities
5. Famous events from history which parallel or repeat each other.

Add your own:

_____

_____

_____

After doing the nonverbal mirror exercise, players may wish to jump ahead and try some verbal Twists and Turns (Chapter 9).

MACHINES

Hilda enters the circle while the other players eagerly wait their turn. As Hilda's bowed head rises slowly, her hand springs out like that of a policewoman stopping traffic. Head moving to the right, hand to the left, her mouth emits an energetic "Hi!" Suddenly, Stuart's stiffened arm connects with Hilda's bobbing hand. "Shalom, shalom," he intones, spacing the words between Hilda's "hi's." Barbara positions her body between Hilda and Stuart. Her fingers snap in counterpoint to the other sounds as she adds "Bonjour." The creation of an International Greeting Machine is on the way!

And so welcome to the world of machines. Making human machines is an exciting method for developing group

Creating a "Hello Soul" Machine.
(*Photo by Jonathan Ishie*)

communication in creative movement and pantomime. In planning a machine, an individual's vision of the outcome is always revised in terms of what the other members of the group think and do. Once players become attuned to the concept of making machines, creative sparks ignite spontaneously. Ideas are tried out, some accepted, others rejected—to the point where everyone makes a contribution to a mosaic of imagination. As one player observed, "Although each member of a machine has a separate role, everyone must function as a unit. Making machines taught me to work together with others." Another said making machines "creates an atmosphere where everyone is helping each other, so that the result is a group success rather than individuals competing against each other."

Extensive experience in improvisational theater is not really necessary for making machines. In fact, along with the basic trust, relaxation, and concentration games discussed in Chapters 2 and 3, this exercise is an effective way to introduce ensemble playing.

MOTIVATION

There are a number of ways to begin making people machines. Good warm-up games include passing around faces and sounds expressing different emotions and playing mirrors. Also, be aware of your body and the interrelatedness of your limbs. To show how the body can be tensed and relaxed, you can move around the room, first as a stiff toy soldier and then as a limp doll, or be a human puppet manipulated by imaginary strings.

Other ways to start include showing pictures of appliances, futuristic contraptions, or abstract paintings (Picasso's, for example) to stimulate the imaginations of the participants. The group can also discuss briefly the uses and drawbacks of machines and electronics in our daily lives.

A high school class, while reading Toffler's *Future Shock,* made a Disposable-Parts Machine to show that the world was headed for too much change in too little time. A person came into the Miracle Machine Shop for a duplicate part of anything that wore out. The only trouble was, the machine itself wore out and could not be replaced, since it was unique. Reading science fiction stories that show humanity in conflict with machines is also a good motivator for making machines. However, just a single excursion in school, in the neighborhood, or into the world of business should suggest many ideas for machines.

GETTING STARTED

After a *brief* warm-up (a few appropriate exercises from Chapters 1 or 2), we prefer to begin by simply announcing, "Let's make some machines!" First, the workshop is subdivided into equal groups of four, five, or six players, depending on how many there are in the class. Then one group is picked to demonstrate—on the spot—how human machines are made. In order to help the group players relate to one another, the following guidelines are introduced:

1. Every part of the machine should be connected (though not always touching) to at least one other part of the machine.

2. Nearly every part of the machine should move. Use complementary and/or opposing movements.

3. The completed machine should, if possible, accomplish something—we want to see it *do* something.

4. Whenever possible, a variety of spatial levels, stylized movements, and contrapuntal sounds should be explored. Stretch your body and imagination.

5. From here on in, it is a simple case of one person starting a movement and a sound. Then another person comes in and builds on the first player's contribution; then a third player connects with one of the other players. This process continues until the human machine begins to grow and a semblance of form emerges.

After the demonstration, the workshop or class members have a good sense of how machines are made and are ready to explore their own creative efforts.

Younger children (under six) may have numbers assigned to them to help the sequence of building parts of the human machine. For example, a kindergarten teacher reported how her students made a Human Washing Machine. Numbers 1 through 5 became the actual cylindrical machine (with one person as the spindle inside it); No. 6 became the hole where the money goes in; Nos. 7 through 10 became the clothes; 11 and 12, the box of soap; other children, the clotheslines; and so forth.

DEVELOPMENT

No two groups work the same way. Some prefer to spend more time planning; other groups prefer to test their ideas on the floor through trial and error. In most cases, it is a combination of experimentation, discussion, and retesting. Do not worry that the machine may not make exact sense during planning; the "constructive accident" is always to be encouraged during playing. Machines do not have to be perfect,

Student teachers in the process of making a Cuckoo Clock.
(*Photo by Jonathan Ishie*)

CoMixCo, directed by Milton Polsky and Carole Rosen, make a Sun Machine, inspired by Robert U. Taylor's setting.
(*Photo by Peter Munch*)

Students in a summer creative drama workshop conducted by Milton Polsky making a Greeting Machine.
(*Photo by Jonathan Ishie*)

The Patchwork Players make a Human Conveyer Machine during rehearsal.
(*Photo by Harout Merigan*)

either. The important things are group cooperation and creative fun. Making machines develops

- Concentration
- Coordination
- Cooperation

Said one player about the exercise: "It's fun to see what it's like to be an inanimate object, but it also lets you see what extreme cooperation between precise actions feels like."

Whatever combination of process is utilized, the creative products that emerge are absolutely amazing: multileveled typewriters with shifting human paper, automobiles with moving wheels, electric fans, movie projectors, blenders with pop-up human buttons for different speeds, pinball machines, revolving cuckoo clocks, and a host of machines that do not have any utilitarian function but that are wildly abstract and imaginative concoctions of sound and movement, expressing the essence of an emotion or mood.

One high-school group came up with the ingenious idea of a "French" toaster. A button was pressed, and the sides of the toaster (six students on different spatial levels) first became depressed (physically as well as emotionally). Then the bread (another student) went in, and when the toast finally popped up, the sides tickled it—a very sensual experience. A group of first graders became the inner part of a fine, musical Swiss watch—all intricately interconnected through the media of movement and sound. One of our favorites was the creation of a human potter's wheel. As different pieces of clay (students) were whirled around by a centrifugal force, the clay was molded into whatever object the player desired, as long as it was expressed in fantasy mime (Chapter 6). Other groups have made imaginative car washes, "soul" machines, and record players with different speeds so that a (human) record could be placed on the spindle.

As you can see, it is fun to leave spaces in the machine so that individuals going through them can be qualitatively changed into something else: a human piece of ice going through a number of changes in a blender, for example, or combinations of people ingredients coming out as a cake from a Pastry Machine. Someone can become the ball being bounced back and forth by the parts of a human pinball machine. It is also fun to slow down and speed up a machine, have it go in different directions, possibly even break down. Explore different levels of switches, levers, and buttons . . . and all kinds of sounds, including gibberish.

USES

IN THE THEATER

Machines, called "part of a whole," by Viola Spolin, are often used in the theater.* One student director explained to her cast: "Each member of a cast is like a part of a machine, a part without which the machine can't operate and which can't

* Spolin, p. 73.

The Dance of the Machines, directed by Nikolai Foregger in 1923.
(*Photo courtesy of Mel Gordon*)

operate itself without the machine." Machines can be used to help understand character, mood, and conflict in any scripted play.

Directors employing machines in their presentations may wish to refer to the work of Nikolai Foregger (1892–1939), a Soviet director who produced his most famous creation, *The Dance of the Machines*, in 1923. According to Mel Gordon, the dance was "essentially a revue of various machines portraying the industrial process, each group enacting the movements of gears, levers, fly-wheels, motors, etc."* The geometrical gestures became partial functions of a total rhythmic movement, which was universal.

The Proposition Circus, an improvisational group that performs for children, makes highly stylized Feeling Machines (sad, angry, happy, etc.) based on suggestions supplied by the audience. One of my graduate school theater companies made Weather Machines as part of their musical newspaper revue called *Hot Headlines*. The cast members asked the audience their favorite weather; depending on the responses they proceeded to make a sun, rain, or snow machine—whatever captured the essence of the season. Background piano music enhanced the fantasy feeling for all the machines. The Patchwork Players, a children's theater company, made a giant Traveling Machine as a means to find the land of Honah Lee, where Puff the Magic Dragon lives. The Traveling Machine was comprised of different modes of transportation suggested by the audience. The improvisational ensembles of Archaesus Productions, a talented theater company based in Washington, D.C. (which also conducts workshops in schools), include an Environmental Machine in their repertory. The actors ask the audience to suggest a person, a color, a sound, a smell, and a building. The group builds a machine upon receiving each suggestion; for example, a Martian, green, creaky, a rose, and a skyscraper. After the machine is built, one of the actors asks the audience to change some parts of the machine.

IN THE CLASSROOM

A nursing class led by Nancy Taylor made a Heart Machine. (Players represented the opening and closing of the

* Mel Gordon, "Foregger and the Dance of the Machines," *The Drama Review*, Vol. 19, No. 1 (March 1975), p. 72.

four heart valves with corresponding sounds. Each subgroup created its own version of this Heart Machine; members were able to explore one another's machines by going through them. One group became the "reds" and another, the "blues," thus forming a Circulatory Machine. The players touched fingertips, showing capillaries in the chest organs, liver circulation, and so forth. Afterward, the nursing students were better able to trace blood through their own circulatory systems. One student created a Respiratory Machine with young children—a giant lung, showing how air is exchanged in the blood as the lung inflates and how carbon dioxide is released when the lung deflates.

Machines are fun to use with holiday happenings. During our St. Valentine's Day "Love-In" for young children, one of our theater workshops made a giant Toy Machine. The children were "processed" through the machine and came out as their favorite wind-up, rag doll, or robot toy. During a Halloween "Scare-In" one year, we made a Ghost Machine, through which invited children crawled and jumped, shaking with laughter. In Central Park during the spring, we put together a fantastic Pollution Machine consisting of human smokestacks, with coughs juxtaposed with frightening noise pollutants—the whole thing a hopeless collage of human contamination and waste.

In history and social studies, players can recreate Fulton's steamboat, Morse's telegraph, and Whitney's cotton gin. These, in turn, may be contrasted with such modern inventions as the telephone, airplanes, and spacecraft, relating historical periods and social conditions, including the Industrial Revolution, the transformation of nature into energy, and preoccupation with power. If a machine consumes more energy than it expends, the waste is expressed in friction. How is this related to human nature?

ROLE-PLAYING

In diverse role-playing situations, the use of electromechanical ideas can help us to understand our own strivings and shortcomings better. A case in point is Scooter the Human Computer, an electronic brain of the future that was constructed by students who were discussing various contemporary social problems. Scooter was supposed to digest and analyze important data.

One-half of the class comprised the human computer, and the remainder of the group role-played various people who were waiting expectantly for answers to crucial questions they fed the machine. Some of the problems discussed included the legalization of marijuana, campus cohabitation, and questions of law and order. When intergroup conflicts reached the proportions of crisis, Scooter was "rolled in" to save the day. The questions were fed into an aperture formed by four cupped hands and then passed along a multilevel assembly line.

Scooter's intricate parts were spontaneously added, one at a time, as arms and hands (fingers, too!) performed stylized, expressionistic movements. As the question of how the legalization of pot would affect standards of morality was fed into the machine, one player's arm made a large sweeping arc to the right, feeding the question to a girl's hand, which made a jerking up-and-down motion, connecting to another player, as the imaginary slip of paper passed through the interlinking parts of the machine. Weird whistling sounds and contrapuntal beeps and grunts suggested that the brain of the future was going berserk! The collective Scooter huffed and puffed, whirled and twirled in the process of intricately passing the paper from one limb to another. Then the reverse process was repeated as the answer came back to the human aperture and fell out. The reply (said by Scooter in choral unison): "Overprogrammed—blank–blank—overprogrammed—blank–blank —overprogrammed, etc."

After Scooter the Human Computer broke down, the players had no recourse but to rely on their first computers— their brains. Discussion, debate, and role reversal did not yield perfect solutions to their questions, but human-made problems were aired on a human level involving feelings.

PREMISES FOR SKITS ON MACHINE THEMES

1. Create an International Greeting Machine that breaks down and gets back together.

2. Create a giant Archaeology Machine that reassembles bone fossils of a prehistoric dinosaur.

3. Create an Antipollution Recycling Machine.

4. Create a Parts-of-a-Sentence Machine, the words of which are first scrambled.

5. Create a giant Rock-Crushing Machine, and crush rocks to build a fortress.

6. Create a Soul Machine that becomes the star of a Saturday night dance.

7. Create a Brotherhood or Sisterhood Machine for Brotherhood/Sisterhood Week.

8. Create a Galaxy or Planet Machine.

9. Make a Sound Machine that captures the essence of the sea.

10. Create some important invention such as a cotton gin, reaper, telegraph, telephone, car assembly line, airplane. Show how it works, and run it for the rest of the group.

11. Create a Mean Machine that turns people into creatures of various sorts.

12. Make a Money Machine and divide into groups. Show the different things money can buy to help or hinder society.

It is always fun to devise improvs that have machines as their focal point. In planning these skits, players should think of a simple conflict or dramatic action that will sustain interest. For example, an evil shop manager wants to destroy the Toy Machine, but the manufactured toys plot to foil him. Another example: Four different Exercise Machines vie for the attention of a health advocate and almost wear down from showing off until he decides he needs them all. A final example: A Youth Restorer Machine breaks down and must be repaired by another, larger Restorer Machine.

MORE MARVELOUS MACHINES
- A Printing Press (which makes a favorite newspaper or book)
- A Xerox Machine (which makes gossipy homemade copies)
- A Telegraph (which sends out mysterious messages)
- A Sewing Machine (which makes all kinds of magical clothing)

- A Typewriter (which creates fantastic stories and poems)
- A Light Bulb (which illuminates all kinds of great ideas)
- A Recorder (which duplicates familiar and fantasy sounds)
- A Television Camera (black and white and color, too!)

Add your own:

_____

_____

_____

Whether you use machines in the theater or the classroom, you will find that none can be built without imagination and teamwork. Machines are fun, and they develop purposeful spontaneity. This exercise can be integrated with almost any curriculum content or can stand as an artistic expression in itself. As Scooter would say: Make a machine! And have fun "running" it for others to see!

SEQUENCE: *THE 1–2–3 WARM-UP*

MEDITATION (ALL BY YOURSELF)
Become lost in your own thoughts and feelings as you actively *concentrate* on saying some word over and over to yourself; completely relax. After five minutes or so, *slowly* rise, blink your eyes several times, make contact with another player.

MIRRORS (TWOS AND THREES)
Now start to communicate with that other player. Look into each other's eyes, slowly and intently. Turn your heads into TV cameras, and go in for a close-up; pan your heads to the right and left, and do some long tracking shots, backing away from each other but still mirroring at long distances. In short, be playful. Try variations of the mirror with as many different people as time allows (about three to five minutes); end with a three-person mirror.

Meditation
(*Photo by Alex Gersznowicz*)

Mirrors
(*Photo by Alex Gersznowicz*)

Machines
(*Photo by Alex Gersznowicz*)

MACHINES (THREE OR MORE)

At an agreed-upon signal, there should be a *natural* transition from a three-person mirror into a small-group machine. If there is time, make machines work with different groups consisting of three people.

This warm-up is a very effective way for players to get in touch with themselves and *one another* at the start of a class or before performing a show. The natural transition is from concentration to communication, ending with an act of creation.

PLAYER'S DIARY

1. How did it feel to be a mirror?
2. What did you enjoy mirroring the most? Why?
3. What did you enjoy mirroring the least? Why?

4. How did it feel to be a machine? Or part of one?

5. What was your favorite machine you helped to create? Why?

6. Of the machines you saw, what was your favorite? Why?

7. What do machines and humans have in common?

8. In what ways are machines and humans different?

9. What do mirrors and machines have in common?

10. How are they unlike?

Add your own questions, thoughts, and observations.

ACTION MIME 5

Have you ever felt like becoming a bird soaring through the sky? A bear crawling through a cave? A tired sailor rowing against the wind in a storm? A robot on a rampage? A parent struggling up twelve flights of stairs with heavy bundles of groceries? Do you remember expressing such feelings with your body?

Most likely, as a young child, you often acted out these feelings without thinking about how to do it. At that time, you entered freely into the world of fantasy, becoming whatever you wanted to, whenever you wanted to. Using your body was a natural form of expression, and you spontaneously acted out almost anything that made a strong impression on you— whether it reflected your everyday experiences or originated in the world of fantasy or imagination. Through such play, much of your fantasy world comes into closer harmony with the world around you.

THE SHAPES OF SILENCE

In much of the make-believe world you created as a child, you probably did not use words to express what was in your mind. When you recreated the "real" world of adults in the course of your playacting, you used a minimum of props or none at all. A real bag of groceries, a real boat, and other objects were unnecessary for dramatic play. You probably did not have such objects or props readily accessible. It was also more challenging to make what was happening in the imagination become visible to others simply through body movements and gestures. So, in place of talking and using real objects, you often substituted body actions to create characters, tell a story, or help unfold a scene or situation from life or literature. In short, you were actively involved in *action mime*, the oldest human language. Action mime—the visual language of silence—is a way of expressing feelings and ideas through the body and of communicating these thoughts and emotions to others.

JUST FOR STARTERS

You can start with simple pantomime activities involving large and small movements. For example:

1. Tie your shoelaces.
2. Empty out a garbage can.
3. Brush your teeth.
4. Eat some spaghetti.
5. Eat some chewy cashew nuts.
6. Shovel some snow.
7. Crack an egg.
8. Rake some leaves.
9. Put a coin into the Coke machine.
10. Eat some spaghetti.

Always be aware of an object's surface (shape, size, and texture) and weight.
(*Photo by Hernando Gonzalez*)

When pantomiming simple objects, it is always helpful to make a mental picture of what you are doing, paying special attention to the object's *surface* (*shape, size,* and *texture*) and *weight.*

HINTS FOR THE PLAYERS

While performing simple action pantomime, the image that originates in your mind should be clearly indicated by the appropriate action. If you are shoveling snow, for example, make sure the shovel remains constant in its size, shape, and weight and that it does·not slip from your hands and wander around aimlessly in the air. Define the shape and boundaries of the shovel so that its movements can be followed clearly in the movements of your hands.

It is often helpful to compare the object you are pantomiming with its real counterpart, if available. For example, lift and swing a real shovel, and then do it in pantomime. What differences do you notice between handling the real and the imaginary objects? Pantomime work becomes more convincing when you believe in what you are doing and endow your object with a personality. Ask yourself:

1. How do I feel when I shovel snow? Am I tired, cold, happy, annoyed, or what? Pick one element of mood, and show this in how you perform the action.
2. Am I communicating this feeling through my actions?
3. Have I shown with every fiber of my imagination and body what I am attempting to do?

SIMPLE PANTOMIME ACTIONS (CARD GAME)

List ten tasks involving some simple action. Write each task on a single card. Distribute the cards, and ask for volunteers to perform them. After the volunteer has indicated that the pantomime is completed by raising his or her hand, the rest of the participants can guess the activity that was pantomimed. This ground rule should be carefully observed, because the players' concentration will be broken if the guessing starts prematurely.

Pantomime is easy when you know the ropes. Just ask the Patchwork Players. (*Photo courtesy of the Patchwork Players.*)

"Avner the Eccentric", old world clown
in action.

(Photo by Peter Kent)

VARIATIONS

1. The participants as a group enact one *individual* task. For example, everyone is shoveling snow. Someone calls out a series of adverbs, such as

quickly	sloppily
lazily	slowly
smoothly	numbly
jerkily	cheerfully

The players go through the series of changes indicated by the particular adverb cue.

2. The group enacts a *sharing* activity, such as eating an outdoor picnic lunch. All the actions associated with eating lunch are performed one at a time, such as spreading the blankets, putting down the baskets, taking out the food, setting the places, and so on. Carefully make a mental picture of the place before you. Outline the dimensions of the plates, forks, knives, glasses, and so forth, and start eating the picnic lunch. After a few moments, each participant can share his or her particular food with the neighbor on the right. Success will be indicated when each player can communicate *clearly* what is being passed around and eaten. After a while, a communal meal can develop, with everyone in the circle sharing one another's food. These group sharing activities can include familiar actions using a *variety of levels*. For example:

SITTING

eating	watching a sporting
schooling	event
watching a movie	visiting a friend

Add your own:

_____   _____

_____   _____

_____   _____

STANDING

making a snowman	throwing a snowball
throwing a ball	putting on a tie
reading information on a	tying a knot
mailbox	picking a flower

Add your own:

_____   _____

_____   _____

MOVING

skating	playing tennis
helping people up the	playing volleyball
stairs	playing basketball
moving furniture	marching in a parade

Add your own:

_____   _____

_____   _____

3. Another variation is to add an adjective that expresses a *mood:* For example, while eating a picnic lunch, you are fussy, hungry, filled-up, messy, and so forth. Still another variation is to change the seasonal elements. Perhaps you are eating your lunch while the sun is out, and you feel warm and good all over. Now, suddenly, the wind begins to blow, clouds cover the sun, and it becomes chilly. It is beginning to rain; after a while the rain turns to sleet and then to thick snow. How does *each* seasonal change affect your actions? How do you feel when it begins to snow, and what do you do?

PANTOMIME IN PAIRS

LAND, SEA, AND SKY
1. The group counts off randomly in 1s and 2s.
2. All the 1s form an inner circle.
3. The 2s form a circle around the 1s.
4. On cue of the leader, the 1s move in a clockwise direction, and the 2s move in a counterclockwise direction.

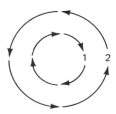

5. After ten seconds or so, the leader calls out "Stop!"
6. A player from the 1 circle will be automatically lined up with a player from the 2 circle, and they exchange a simple activity. For example, two players may share such actions such as sharing food, baking a cake, playing tennis, and so on.

7. The leader can call out a particular place (such as land, sea, or sky) or a time of day or a season, and the two players lined up with each other perform an appropriate pantomime activity connected with the words called out. For example, if the leader calls out "sea," Player 1 could be a lifeguard saving Player 2 from drowning. If the leader calls out "land," Player 2 could be helping Player 1 put on skis. The leader can vary the actions by calling out strenuous and/or light activities such as choppng wood or sweeping the floor. Activity can be further varied by calling out specialized tasks such as those of an artist (painting, etching, coloring) contrasted with those of a laborer doing heavy work (drilling, laying bricks, lifting boxes) and comparing the movements. Whatever mime is involved, take time to make the actions *clear*. For example, if you find a stray kitten, think about its particular surface (size, shape, and texture) and weight. What do you feed it? How much or little food? How do you carry it? Is the kitty distracted by any-thing—a noise, a dog, another cat, trying to stay awake?

Playing musical instruments—can you guess which ones?
(*Photo courtesy of the Proposition Circus, directed by Allan Albert.*)

Batter up!
(*Photo courtesy of the Street 70 Mime Troop*)

Watch the tee. . . .
(*Photo by Leonard Lewis*)

1. Two groups are formed by counting off in 1s and 2s.

2. The two groups line up in two straight lines on either side of the room.

3. The leader calls out a simple pantomime activity involving a definite movement, such as "play ball!" or "cross the street."

4. A player from each side proceeds to perform the pantomime activity while moving toward an imaginary line drawn across the center of the room.

5. At this midway point, Player 1 takes over Player 2's movements and vice versa. For example, Player 1 playing tennis takes over Player 2's baseball actions and vice versa.

GROUP ACTION MIME

WHAT'S YOUR TRADE?

1. Two groups are formed by counting off in 1s and 2s.

2. The two groups both form huddles and decide on an occupation that involves clear and definite action. For example, the 1s might decide to become hospital workers, whereas the 2s might decide to be clock makers.

3. After each group decides what its occupation will be, it lines up once again, ready to advance toward an imaginary center line as follows:

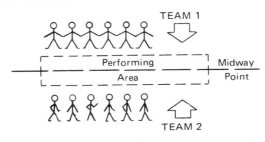

TEAM 1: *Here we come!* (advances one step)

TEAM 2: *Where are you from?* (advances one step)

TEAM 1: [*name of your city or town*] (advances one step)

TEAM 2: *What's your trade?* (advances one step)

TEAM 1: *Lemonade.* (advances one step)

TEAM 2: *Show us some!* (advances one step)

Team 1 now proceeds to act out in pantomime the trade of hospital workers. Some may be orderlies, some may be doctors and nurses, some may be doing laboratory work as blood samplers; perhaps two players are an intravenous feeding setup running into another player's arm. No talking permitted, but sounds may be used.

4. As soon as the trade is correctly guessed by Team 2, the Team 1 players run back to home base, with Team 2 players in pursuit.

5. The Team 1 players who are tagged join Team 2.

6. Team 2 now proceeds to act out their pantomime—for example, clock makers—following the method of advancing in step 3.

7. New occupations are chosen by each team, and the game continues. As a variation, the two teams can proceed to the center line in slow motion; the trades can also be enacted in slow motion. The leader can also "command" the players to advance toward the centerline in baby steps, one leg up, hopping, etc.

MATCH THE PAIR (CARD GAME)

Prepare a series of cards with one object written or illustrated on each card. The cards can depict such familiar items as:

book	snail
hammer	earring
sand	nail
peach	face

Each player matches up two of the prepared pictures. For example, one participant may match the hammer and nails. He or she then proceeds to pantomime this activity. The task is completed when the player has communicated to the others that he or she is pounding a nail with a hammer. The rest of the players guess the activity when the player signals completion by holding up his or her right hand.

I OBJECT TO THE OBJECT

1. Discuss objects in your lives that have not worked properly or that have malfunctioned on occasion. Examples include:

- Jelly doughnuts that squirt jelly on your shirt.
- Wire hangers that scratch you.
- Spray cans that don't spray.
- Aspirin bottles that don't open.
- Shoes that are too small or too large.

Add your own:

_____

_____

_____

2. Divide into four or five groups. Each group enacts a short pantomime centering around one objectionable object. Each group decides upon the characters, the central conflict, and how it will be resolved. For example, in one group portraying a family at breakfast, the youngest member of the family created an invisible machine that made people and objects disappear. A jelly doughnut was eaten while it was in this state of tele-transportation, leaving no jelly stains on his shirt.

THE HAUNTED HOUSE

1. Make a list of weird objects and characters that might be found in a haunted house high on a hill in Weirdsville.

Objecting to bottles that won't open.
(Photo by Terry Buchalter)

Through a strange process of telekinesis, the objects are seen in one place and then reappear in another a few seconds later.

2. Workshop members take turns describing where the mysterious objects have floated to and try to pick them up before the objects get away. This exercise is guaranteed to send chills up and down the spine!

PANTOMIME PLAYS FROM PICTURES

1. Prepare a series of pictures cut out from magazines and newspapers, and mount them on cardboard. These pictures can be commercials, announcements, illustrations, drawings, and paintings. Picture ideas can also come right from T-shirts the players are wearing. Preferably, the pictures should contain no words or very few words.

2. The group discusses the picture and then proceeds to enact a pantomime skit that has been triggered off by the picture. Examples of pictures include a little girl blowing out some candles; a teenager writing on a blackboard; an old man sharpening a pencil; a chicken being hatched from an egg while holding an American flag (the ad for the musical *1776*); a lion roaming the streets (the ad for Dreyfus growth stocks). The concept of pictures also can be extended to buttons that have pictures on them or a word or two, such as "People Pollute," "Peace," "Don't Be Fuelish," etc.

GIBBERISH INTERVIEWS (GIBBERVIEWS)

You are at a cocktail party, airport, or TV station interviewing a celebrity from a foreign country. An interesting variation is for one player to be a reporter or interviewer asking the celebrity questions in English. The celebrity responds in gibberish (nonsense syllables), capturing the essence of the native tongue (Italian -*a* and -*o* endings, Chinese -*ings*, Russian hard *k*s and rolling *r*s, for example) and gesturing in pantomime. An interpreter who speaks the same native language translates the reporter's questions into gibberish and in turn translates the celebrity's responses into English for the reporter. An example of how a "gibberview" might start:

REPORTER (miming talking into microphone): *Hello, ladies and gentlemen out there in TV-land. This is Milton Mildew giving you an on-the-spot scoop interview with Powerful Paul, reputedly one of the strongest men on*

A magazine ad can trigger a pantomime skit.
(*Courtesy of Forbes Magazine*)

The three monkeys are giving the American corporation a bad name.

See no evil. Hear no evil. Speak no evil.

Woe betide the Board of Directors guided by those famous turn-off traits.

When they pretend not to notice such corporate evils as bribery, illegal campaign contributions and payoffs—you know what is then likely to happen.

Out of such monkeyshines—headlines happen. Heads roll. Corporations founder.

Out of such scandals, questions arise. How did these corporate evils go by the board? Why didn't they see the consequences? Why didn't they hear the warning signals? Why didn't they speak up?

"Will the Directors Speak Up?" was a recent cover story in Forbes Magazine. To probe for answers, Forbes dug into the history of how boards began. Examined the legal liabilities of being a director. Even sat in on an actual corporate board meeting.

Can you imagine America's corporate officers and directors giving Forbes articles, such as this one, anything less than their undivided attention? And that's

how it is, issue after issue. That's the kind of wide-awake, editorial vitality that's put Forbes way out front in the measured reading preferences of America's top management.

Once again verification of this leadership-readership was provided when the research firm of Erdos and Morgan, Inc. made a reconfirming study of corporate officer reading preferences among 1300 of America's largest companies.

The results showed Forbes to be read by more top management executives than any of the other major business or news magazines. Here are the percentages, based on magazines read regularly:

Forbes	78.7%
Business Week	64.0%
Fortune	46.6%
Time	45.5%
Newsweek	32.3%
U.S. News & World Report	28.2%

No wonder Forbes was the *only* leading business or news magazine up in advertising pages in 1975.

Which means that our gains for the first six months of 1976 were gains over *gains*—not simply recovery figures.

And we're up 156 pages in the first half of 1976. That's an unprecedented 21% over the same period in record-breaking 1975.

Why? Because of the quality and intensity of our readership.

Because Forbes is *counted on* to see, hear and speak right out about whatever's going on. Without glossing over the facts.

Without monkeying around.

FORBES: CAPITALIST TOOL

Earth, just back from the Olympics held in his native country of Argentina. How are you feeling, Paul?

INTERPRETER (turning to Paul): *Esa capatu saloong ta-roo?*

STRONG MAN (flexing his muscles and pushing out his chest): *Oo, capatu saloong osta quanto rabuta lavornia ost latora requesta botta mano, eas ta quanto sabada.*

INTERPRETER (turning to reporter): *He says he's shy.*

REPORTER: *Really? Would you kindly ask him how he likes this country?*

INTERPRETER: *Esa maronna besaqua ista beel ah, Americasiona, quanto rax ala bala?*

STRONG MAN (pantomiming outline of tall buildings, zooming cars, plugging his ears with fingers; in a loud voice): *Oosa, maka rebozo sa toob! Toob. Oos louda samonga!*

INTERPRETER: *He likes everything, except the . . .*

REPORTER: *Except what?*

STRONG MAN (miming an airplane): *Toob! Toob!*

INTERPRETER: *The noise, the noise. He says the plane and everything makes too much noise.*

REPORTER: *Oh, I see. . . .*

The foreign celebrity is shocked at the interviewer's question. The translator is in the middle in this Gibberview.

(*Photo by Claudia M. Caruana*)

TECHNIQUE FOR LEARNING GIBBERISH

1. After playing "Circle Story" (discussed in Chapter 6 under "Personal Stories, Myths, and Dreams"), continue to tell stories by throwing the ball to each other. But this time tell the story in gibberish, using inflections of voice and plenty of body language.

2. After a few minutes of storytelling (everyone should have a chance to make a contribution to the story), players can rise and walk or run around the room. Upon the signal of the leader, or anyone in the group, stop walking and—in gibberish—tell the person next to you something funny that happened to you for about thirty seconds. Then listen to your partner's tale. Now continue to walk around the room some more until you get another signal to stop. This time, with a new partner, exchange something sad in gibberish; the next time around, perhaps, share an invention, or have an angry exchange of words (all in fun, of course). In no time at all, you will have gotten the knack of gibberish and have a great time, as well, with a wonderful outpouring of positive energy.

One student expressed her fondness for gibberish as follows: "I used to do this when I was young, playing house with my brothers and sisters. We'd make up our own language—in this session, we were able to really communicate and understand each other ... gestures helped so much!" Ozimanda parada peru!

PLAYING ROLES IN PANTOMIME

Acting out a variety of social roles from real life and literature enables us to put ourselves in the shoes of another person to better understand what he or she is feeling and thinking. Role-playing on a social level helps people become more sensitive to one another. Old roles from the past are reexamined, and new roles are "tried on" in a supportive atmosphere that encourages creative thinking and a healthy respect for sharing ideas.

A CIRCLE OF COMMUNITY CHARACTERS

A social role is a person's place in the community; the fleshing out of that role with particular traits is characterization. Every community has its assortment of interesting characters—for example, the news dealer, pushcart salesperson, pizza maker, and so on.

Form three or four groups of five players each. Each member of the group recalls and/or observes in *detail* one or two characters in the community and improvises their significant actions. Afterward, the group members discuss the dominant traits of the person observed. In the discussion, isolate the character's special way of speaking, standing, walking, and gesturing. Whenever possible, discuss cultural determinants as a way of sensing that an understanding of cultural differences can break down social barriers between people.

1. Each player assumes the role of someone in the community—for example:

an elevator operator	a waiter
a schoolteacher	a TV personality
a store clerk	a laborer

Add your own:

_____	_____
_____	_____
_____	_____

2. The rest of the players in the circle ask questions of the character, who must then enact some significant aspect of his or her occupation. Then the occupational role is guessed. How did the players know who the character was?

3. As a variation, each player can give a brief characterization of a favorite person or one they would most like to be. The group then guesses the various characters.

TRYING ON ROLES

1. Prepare two stacks of 9 × 14 cards (cardboard from laundered shirts is ideal). Print the following roles in large block letters on the cards:

STACK 1	STACK 2
Teacher	Student
Salesperson	Customer
Police Officer	Criminal
Manager	Worker
_____	_____
_____	_____

2. The cards are distributed at random to be worn around the necks of the players.

3. All players move around the room so that the cards become mixed.

4. At an appropriate signal, players attempt to match up roles—for example, *salesperson* and *customer.*

5. Each pair takes a few minutes to work out a little skit that has a problem and a solution in it. For example, the salesperson wants to sell the customer a pair of shoes; the customer wants to take some time about the selection.

6. If there is time, reverse roles.

THAT IS MY HAT!

1. Players collect a bag or box of hats worn by members of the community designating such occupational roles as the following:

fire chief	mail carrier
police officer	sanitation worker

2. Each player takes a hat and becomes the character associated with it; the group as a whole (or working in smaller groups) prepares a five-minute skit that has a beginning, middle, and end. At all times, remember:

- *Who* you are,
- *What* your action is in the skit, and
- *Where* you are.

Try your own variations, such as "Shoes Are the Clues." Simply bring in way-out pictures of shoes (police, cowboy,

A bag of hats triggers a dramatic scene at the Stuyvesant Adult Center Dramatic Group.
(*Photo by Alex Gersznowicz*)

Alice and the Mad Hatter in a playful burlesque exchange of hats, props, and dialogue. A feather duster becomes a gun; an umbrella transforms into a sword.
(*Photo by John Traversa, Metro Theater Circus.*)

space, and so on), and become characters associated with them; work out a little scene. Afterwards the group can discuss the following:

1. What was the central problem or control?
2. What was each person's role in the problem?
3. How was the problem solved? How could/should the conflict have been resolved?

For example, three sisters are playing with their brother, who suddenly begins to bother them. What are the alternative actions? The brother could learn to play with them; he could go outside and play; he could be punished. Are there additional characters needed to complete the scene? Who? Where are they needed, and what will they do? Draw out as many clues as you need to become nosey "Drama Detectives."

PICK-A-PLACE

1. Form three or four subgroups consisting of about five players each.

2. Each group decides on a very specific place where they would like to be to explore. Examples include the following:

a planetarium	a supermarket
a sports stadium	a restaurant

3. Create a situation in the particular place chosen.

COMMON TASK

The group members choose a common task, such as trying on a new suit in a clothing store, decorating a cake, packing a box, looking for a book in the library—but all as *different* characters. How does being the different characters, such as a boxer, dancer, laborer, office worker, affect the task being enacted?

COMMON PLACE

The group picks a familiar place (such as a street) or a fantastic place (such as a magic alley) and dramatizes the player's interpretation of the character's action in the place. For example, an older man hobbling across a busy street or moving cautiously; a child carelessly darting across a busy street, running in and out in front of cars; a dating couple holding hands, moving across the street starry-eyed.

SPECIAL PLACE

Ironically, nonverbal exploration often leads to dynamic discussions that explore common feelings and cultural differences that can be shared. Here is an example:

JAPANESE TEA CEREMONY

Pair off players around a circle. In each pair, one player is the Host, and the other is the Guest. Host and Guest face each other in seated positions on the floor. Guest's hands are folded on his or her lap. Host makes the tea in pantomime as follows:

HOST

1. Graciously folds napkin and gently wipes teacup.

2. Scoops two spoons of tea leaves into the cup.

3. Stirs tea leaves with stirrer.

4. Pours hot water into the cup.

5. Turns the cup three times in hand and leans a little forward to Guest.

6. Serves the tea.

GUEST

1. Takes the teacup in hand, first drinks a small amount in appreciation, and then finishes drinking tea.

2. Returns cup graciously to Host with appreciation. Host and Guest exchange greetings, ending the ceremony.

Add your own ideas for showing customs of different countries in pantomime:

_____

_____

_____

ROLE-PLAYING CHARACTERS FROM LITERATURE

The group imagines it is in the library. It is twelve o'clock. Everyone has gone home. Magically, the characters from favorite books and stories come alive. Enact scenes from stories that have left a strong impression and have captured the imagination of the players, such as:

- Madame Curie making an important discovery in *The Microbe Hunters.*

- The boys discovering the shell conch in *Lord of the Flies.*

- An exciting scene from the *Bible.*

- Sherlock Holmes making an important discovery.

Add your own:

_____

_____

_____

103

ROLE-PLAYING CHARACTERS AND
EVENTS FROM HISTORY

The group enacts events from history. For example, for Puerto Rican Discovery Week, players could enact a scene from the life of the Tainos Indians and how the party of Colón (Columbus) treated them after invading their island. The group might show young Frederick Douglass resisting his slave master and eventually running away disguised as a sailor; Marconi, against great odds, discovering the wireless; George Sand coping with the pressure of society, planning her next book; and so forth. It is a good idea for the class to keep a special drama box or file for different subjects.

A DAY IN THE LIFETIME

1. The entire group decides on a famous personality from history, literature, or modern-day life to improvise. The dominant traits, weaknesses, strengths, contributions, and eccentricities of this personality are then discussed.

2. Four or five subgroups are formed, with each group improvising a day in the lifetime of the personality, with such divisions as early formative years, turning point, and later years.

3. Variations include breaking down one day—morning, noon, night—of decision in the life of the character. Players become other characters in the personality's life, as well as the objects and environments encountered during that particular day.

For example, a group broke up into five groups and improvised five stages in the life of abolitionist Frederick Douglass: (a) his early life as a slave; (b) resisting the physical and mental brutality of a slave-breaker when he was a teenager; (c) running away from slavery; (d) becoming an abolitionist speaker and fighter for freedom; and (e) his later life as Minister to Haiti.

EVALUATION

After each skit, a brief discussion can take place, with the leader and group covering the following guidelines. Players

Pantomime can be effective on stage, as in this scene with Joe Morton (and *Raisin* Company) making a phone call on his way to work.
(*Photo courtesy of Max Eisen*)

... as well as in the recreation center, where members of a senior center mime planting seeds and gathering the garden.
(*Photo by Terry Buchalter, courtesy of Brookdale Drama Project.*)

should take turns leading the evaluation. *Do not* forget to discuss important awareness values: (1) Did the group members use their imaginations? In which *specific* ways? (2) Was there cooperation? Specifically, how was this shown? Using the guidelines of ACTED ST (ACTED STORY), discuss:

- *Action:* Was it clear? Too much? Too little?
- Characters: Were they believable? Why? Why not?
- *Timing:* Did it follow a natural pace? Too much exposition in the beginning? Did the ending drag out?
- *Environment:* Did the actors feel a sense of the *where?*
- *Drama:* Were the problem and conflict clear?

- *Situation:* How could it be developed and improved?
- *Teamwork:* Was there cooperation among the players in developing the skit? Did they react to one another? Was there give-and-take in developing the scene?

In evaluating the skits, be aware of visual vocabulary and spatial geography—the body's relationship to space and the influence of spatial environment upon our behavior. Players should try to become more aware of the sphere of "social space" around them—why certain people stand farther apart from some people and closer to others—and the influence of cultural factors on these choices.

In respect to nonverbal cues and signals, in which ways are people alike? In which ways are they different? If someone comes into your room right now, and you put this book down and cross your arms over your chest, what does it mean? Are you putting yourself on guard? Are you tired? Are you showing a protective attitude? Naturally, the answers depend on the specific social setting, who came in, emotional states, and many other frames of reference.

In the process of discovering and expressing our emotions, we experience a vital part of what makes us human. Often what we are afraid of expressing can be dealt with when we discover that we're not the only ones with that particular feeling. As one student observed: "It's fun playing people other than myself. . . . In exploring myself through others, I'm learning how much I have in common with other people. . . . People care about what I think and feel . . . this makes me more confident to go on and learn more about myself." How lovely to be able to communicate with each other in a wonderful world of silence, where gestures and movements speak so well.

PLAYER'S DIARY

1. What is your favorite song? Can you act parts of it out?

2. What is your favorite musical instrument? Can you play it in pantomime?

3. Can you describe the happiest day of your life? Can you pantomime one significant action during this day?

4. Can you describe your best friend? Can you act out in pantomime what you like to do with him or her?

5. What is your favorite sport? Can you act it out in pantomime?

6. What is your favorite hobby? Can you act it out in pantomime?

7. What is your favorite food? Can you show how you eat it?

8. What is your favorite foreign food? Can you show how you eat it?

9. Can you act out in pantomime how you go to school? Work? A leisure activity?

10. What is your favorite pantomime activity so far? Why?

Add your own questions, thoughts, and observations.

FANTASY MIME 6

When you thread an imaginary needle, throw an imaginary ball, or play an imaginary piano, you are performing what the last chapter, "Action Mime," was all about. However, when you actually make the needle and thread with your body or become a bouncing ball, or when your group of players becomes a piano, you are then performing *fantasy mime*. It is no great feat for a young child's fancy to turn a parent's pair of crossed legs into a bridge or an outstretched arm into a highway for little cares to rumble over. By stretching the human imagination, all of us can take a beautiful leap into the world of fantasy by letting our bodies become the essence of things and environments.

JUST FOR STARTERS

As usual, it is preferable to start off with some quick icebreakers and warm-ups (see Chapter 1). In this case, group mime

109

sports are especially appropriate. For example, play basketball in mime, or go swimming, or jump rope. Become the great Pelé on the soccer field. Now try these sports with some of the participants actually becoming the long rope, the balls and baskets, the waves in the pool.

WARM-UPS

1. Everyone decides on a type of bizarre creature or form of vegetation.
2. Move bodies while standing in place—stretching, contracting, rising, and sinking.
3. Continue the movement, animating it with one sound.
4. Freeze.
5. Five or six players become chairs and table.
6. The rest become trees and rocks and mushrooms that you would find in an enchanted forest.
7. Create a picnic in the forest. Pass around a favorite food, and actually *become* the ingredients for a few seconds. For example, the pepper jumps quickly up and down; ice cream melts to the ground if the sun is out; the orange wears a bright, broad smile.

Improvise a variation of the song "Old McDonald," becoming the suggested environments. Old McDonald had a:

farm   swamp
woodland   pond
garden   vineyard

Add your own:

_____   _____

_____   _____

_____   _____

In fantasy mime, become your favorite or most unusual possession at home. For example, you might become a fancy salt or pepper shaker, adding "spice" to a human-group salad platter, the parts of which are sprawling all over the floor. Or try this "sticky" situation: You are flypaper hanging from a ceiling trying to catch pesty flies in the room.

BODY WORDS

1. Everyone walks slowly around the room. The leader calls out a variety of words—one at a time—such as:

Peace	School
Morning	Friend
Name of your	Love
city or village	Sun

Add your own:

_____	_____
_____	_____
_____	_____

2. React emotionally to each word, capturing its essence in the body, and then, still standing in place, project the word so that it is physically enlarged. In this exercise, everyone should avoid looking at one another. Make every effort to personalize the situation. When the word is heard, don't think so much about what shape you will give it; just let it flow naturally. Often activity will evolve purpose and direction. Have faith in your inner creativity.

Remember the problem of the centipede—if it had to think about which leg to start off on, it would be paralyzed. During the process of making the work larger— that is, in projecting it—you can think about refining it.

DISCOVER FANTASY MIME OBJECTS

Everyone continues to walk around the room. First, walk around in slow motion. Discover the objects—large and small—in the room, and relate to them as intimately as possible. Personalize the inner life of the object, trying to sense in every possible way the object's surface, its depth, thickness, and potential in motion. Choose one object, and *slowly* become it, drawing out what you consider its essential quality. How does it feel to be a water-basket filling up, or a tablecloth when someone has just spilled hot soup on you? In discovering this essence, search for the difference that makes the difference—the stroke that sets it apart from the other objects in the room. If necessary, work with other players while becoming the object. How does it feel to be two erasers being clapped together?

PERSON, PLACE, THING

After experiencing and becoming several objects, everyone continues walking around the room in pairs. The leader calls out the name of a place: a kitchen, a gym, a library, and so forth. As the place is called out, one player will become an

A fantasy mime bed made by the Patchwork Players.
(*Photo by Alex Gersznowicz*)

object associated with the place and enact a short skit. For example, if *kitchen* is called out, you could become a table or an appliance or a window. Your partner might be eating off the table or putting bread into the toaster. If the place is a toy store, one body or a combination of bodies could become a box and other players, customers. Think to yourself: Is the box small, large, torn, sturdy, rough, smooth, or what? How would I show this in body movement? When the box is picked up, turned over, kicked, dropped, and so on? Can I add a sound that will make my attitude as the box even more convincing? How do I *feel* as a box? How can I show this feeling? If I'm a bench in the park, what *particular* kind of bench could I be?

Create fantasy mime objects associated with the following places:

bus station	doctor's office
police station	classroom
kitchen	movie theater
bank	telephone booth
restaurant	

Add your own:

_____	_____
_____	_____
_____	_____

MOUNTAINS, STREAMS, AND TREES

Group 1: Form a pyramid. You are a mountain range. Your goal is to stand for eternity.

Group 2: Lie down on your backs in a line. Join hands, make and keep contact with the feet of the next person. You are a river, and your goal is to reach the ocean.

Group 3: Each one assumes a different height by sitting, squatting, or standing. Let your arms and feet intertwine. You are vegetation, and your goal is to reach the sun.

After the groups have created their environments, figure out who would inhabit them, and create a skit with a beginning, middle, and end.

It is very important to impart an attitude to the object (or atmosphere) you create with your whole body. For example, when making a tree, decide if you are an old tree or a young sapling, if you are flowery or losing your leaves. When creating the environment, find a space in which the imagination can thrive. With the tree, for example, imagine your seedling sprouting from the ground as it grows into a tree. Then, slowly experience your roots, trunk, branches, and leaves in the surrounding space. In your own mind, react as the tree to:

a warm rain → a tornado → a harsh downpour → a woodpecker → a cool breeze → a lumberjack → a bird's next → a fire.

Add your own:

_____

_____

_____

After experiencing this exercise, one player, Joan Hurowitz, observed:

Improvisation gives you the freedom to try—and to fail— and it gives you an opportunity to see how easily you can break through those inhibitions when you decide to join the group. You move in rather studied gestures. Then without even realizing it, the tree takes on a life of its own, and you begin to feel the weight of those branches, to enjoy the gentle life of the wind, to feel the loss of those leaves, and to know what it feels like to have been standing—firm and solid—for more than a hundred years. You've seen it all. Incredible. The self has become one with nature.

Especially show your emotional reactions with your face. The face is the greatest area of human expression. There are at least eight different ways to smile and six different ways to frown. Indeed, the face is capable of more than a thousand different kinds of expression. How many different ways can

A window in the Play Group, directed by Dennie Cody.
(*Photo by Dennie Cody*)

you twist and contort your face, using the different combinations of facial muscles? Remember to review your inner life: What is it that *you* really want to express? What emotional state produces one of those many expressions?

VARIETY IS ESSENTIAL

1. Vary movement in fantasy mime through speed, size, rhythm, and direction. If possible, use head stands or shoulder stands when appropriate. Yoga positions can be used as well.

2. Add a sound that will complement the rhythmic movement.

3. As a guideline for *self-evaluation*, ask yourself the following question:

> *Have I felt deep within me whatever I wanted to become until it was shown through my arms, my legs, my face, my whole body?*

It is fun to combine the abstract and concrete whenever possible. A college class made up a skit featuring an angry grandfather rocking in a chair (fantasy mime) in a corner. He wanted to play with his grandchildren, who were too busy playing on a rocking chair—three players standing with hands on hips, feet astride, leaning forward with knees stiff and lifting heels from the floor.

MATCH 'EM UP

1. Cards with pictures of different objects are distributed to the entire group.

2. Players become the objects and match 'em up by performing appropriate actions.

brush—comb
cup—saucer
table—chair
hammer—nail

For example, the human hammer will pound the nail, which becomes smaller and smaller as it is hit into another object.

Add your own:

_____   _____

_____   _____

_____   _____

STRANDED

1. Three groups consisting of about a dozen players each are formed.

2. Each group is in a boat, rowing to shore. Suddenly there is a magical thunderstorm, during which the three boats are washed ashore to three different environments: the Arctic, the desert, and a jungle.

3. Half the players become the environment, and the other half try to figure out a way to get off the island.

SOURCE MATERIAL FOR
FANTASY MIME

ORIGINAL STORIES

The greatest resources are original ideas that spring from the imaginations of the players themselves. For example, many exciting skits can evolve from the "Stranded" game. Groups can work together, sharing an incident from real life, or fantasy, or perhaps a dream. The other members of the group can become all the characters, objects, and props in the incident or dream.

Work in groups of five or six players. Each group makes up a story to be acted out in fantasy mime. First, review the *three Ps of play-making:*

- *people*
- *plot*
- *place*

People, in this case, can include animals, birds, or inanimate objects as well. *Plot* is the sequence of incidents that comprise the dramatic action. *Place* is the environment where the dramatic action will happen. While planning the skit, the group decides who is going to do what and where the action will take place. The group may wish to discuss briefly why each character does what he or she does. Stress cooperation and compromise while working on self-created material. Here is a story worked out by one group:

SUN LEAVES
The sun (two players make circle with hands) *shone brightly through the forest* (others in group become trees). *Days passed* (two players walk past each other). *In the middle of a cool blue pond* (trees slowly transform into pool of water by lying on floor with waving, inter-connected arms), *the moon* (two players making the sun transform into the smaller moon) *made a reflection in the pond* (slow-motion mirror). *Days passed again* (two play-

ers walk past each other), *and night fell* (two other players fall and do forward rolls to become winds); *the winds blew* (they add whistling sounds), *and the leaves from the tree fell into the pool of water. A flock of birds* (transformed from trees) *started to sing; the wind stopped to listen while the ground filled up with leaves* (a mosaic of human bodies). *A couple of children came along with a wheelbarrow* (constructed from two or three bodies) *and filled it with leaves. The sun nodded in approval and disappeared.*

EVALUATION CHECKLIST

After the skits have been performed, each group can evaluate its own creation with questions covering the following checklist:

ACTED ST (SHORT FOR ACTED STORY)

- *Action:* Was there too much action? Too little? Believable (even in terms of fantasy)? Why? Why not?

- *Characters:* Were they believable (even as fantasy)? Why? Why not? Was the fantasy mime clearly presented?

- *Timing:* Did the skit follow a natural pace—too much exposition? Too little? Did the ending drag out? Did certain scenes or lines of action outweigh others? Did characters (animate as well as inanimate) *react* to each other?

- *Environment:* Did the actors play a sense of the *where?* Did they incorporate elements of the weather and time of day and seasonal changes?

- *Dialogue:* Was it clear, believable, and consistent with character and story? Too much narration? Too little? How could it be improved?

- *Story:* Was it clear? Consistent with action and characters? How could it be improved?

- *Teamwork:* Did the players work together? Did one actor dominate out of character? Was there give-and-take in developing a scene? How could the ensemble work be improved?

FANTASY

Because fantasy is rooted in truth—no matter how subjective—it can help us to become more aware of life. It is important to discover and distinguish those subjective strands that can express a deeper truth and, in turn, to weave these truths into what can be learned about the real world. Often what is meant to be real may be perceived by a young child as fantasy and vice versa. But everyone, to some degree, learns to control in fantasy a variety of impulses that may be difficult to control in reality. There is a great deal of creative pleasure in exchanging real and make-believe worlds. In this respect, the creation of stories and situations that leap beyond the here and now is a virtue to be nourished rather than grown out of.

FUN WITH FANTASY

1. Each player is asked to name something he or she feels like and why. Examples include: "I feel like a piece of string—because I'm skinny"; "I feel like a jump rope because that's what I want to do." The players act out the responses.

2. Act out a favorite fairy tale in which inanimate objects come alive as personified characters, such as the teapots and darning needles that are endowed with human qualities in some of the stories of Hans Christian Andersen.

3. Mold an extraordinary object out of clay, and then mold the same object with your body.

4. Paint or draw a fantastic scene, and then recreate it with the bodies in your group.

5. Add appropriate sounds to the scene.

6. Take a five-minute magical fantasy trip around the world; go anywhere you like, and do anything you like.

POETRY

Many nursery rhymes, songs, poems, and proverbs lend themselves especially well to fantasy mime enactments. A good example is the nursery rhyme "London Bridge." After it "falls down," you build it up with (human) iron bars; and after the iron bars rust and break, you can build it up once more with sticks and bones. The sticks and bones, too, will tumble down. What will Fair Lady be doing in the in-between time? Another example is Walt Whitman's "There Was a Child Went Forth." The poem begins:

> There was a child went forth every day
> And the first object he look'd upon,
> That object he became,
> And that object became part of him
> For the day or a certain part of the day,
> Or for many years or stretching cycles of years.

You can have fun and stretch your imagination, creating the various objects enumerated in the poem by the narrator: "the early lilacs" ... "the Third-month lambs" ... "the field sprouts" ... and all the various "changes of city and country" life wherever the child goes.

Carl Sandburg's "The Wedding Procession of the Rag Doll and the Broom Handle Who Was in It" includes furnace shovels, spoon lickers, and coffee pots, which can be animated.*

Most good poetry contains a variety of moods, images, and objects that work well with fantasy mime. Some examples from songs include the ice-cream castles in Joni Mitchell's "Clouds," Blood, Sweat and Tears' colorful imagery of painted ponies and flying spinning wheels, and Bob Dylan's "Blowin' in the Wind." In Tom Glazer's "On Top of Spaghetti," humorously delicious images for fantasy mime come into play: the poor meatball rolling off the table onto the floor—then out the door—then into a garden and under a bush. After the

---

* Carl Sandburg, The Wedding Procession of the Rag Doll and the Broom Handle Who Was in It. (New York: Harcourt Brace Jovanovich, 1922).

mushed-up meatball grows into a tree, the tree becomes covered with beautiful moss—more meatballs growing into tomato sauce.

PLAYING POETRY

Act out "The Creation" (a black sermon) by James Weldon Johnson. Use a narrator or choral narration while the group acts out the poem in activity and fantasy mime. Smaller subgroups can act out different stanzas. A sample:

> *Then God reached out and took the light in His hands,*
> *And God rolled the light around in His hands*
> *Until He made the sun;*
> *And He set that sun a-blazing in the heavens.*
> *And the light that was left from making the sun*
> *God gathered it up in a shining ball*
> *And flung it against the darkness,*
> *Spangling the night with the moon and stars*
> *Then down between*
> *The darkness and the light*
> *He hurled the world;*
> *And God said: That's good.**

Act out "Solomon Grundy." Here is an interesting metamorphosis from cradle to coffin:

> *Solomon Grundy, born on Monday* (ensemble makes cradle)
> *Christened on Tuesday* (imaginary font for baptismal rites)
> *Married on Wednesday* (well-wishers shower tapes of confetti; steepled church)
> *Took ill on Thursday* (human bed and flower vase)
> *Died on Saturday* (human hole)
> *Buried on Sunday* (human coffin)
> (This, of course, ends the life of Solomon Grundy.)

Create the central object in the following finger play, using the *whole* body.

---

* Excerpts from "The Creation," from *God's Trombones* by James Weldon Johnson. Copyright 1927 by The Viking Press, Inc. © renewed 1955 by Grace Nail Johnson. Reprinted by permission of Viking Penguin Inc.

I'm a little teapot
Short and stout
Here is my handle
Here is my spout.
When I get all steamed up,
Then I shout—
Just tip me over
And pour me out!

Creative drama students pouring tea into a cup.
(*Photo by Harout Merigan*)

Now add other companion objects for the teapot, which you might find in the kitchen. Create a short pantomime skit.

PROVERBS IN PANTOMIME

Act out the following, combining action and fantasy mime:

1. An empty sack cannot stand up. (*Russian*)
2. Rotten wood cannot be carved. (*Chinese*)
3. When one door shuts, another opens. (*Spanish*)
4. A small hole can sink a big ship. (*Russian*)
5. One pound of learning requires ten pounds of common sense to apply it. (*Persian*)

6. When the fruit is scarcest, its taste is sweetest. (*Irish*)
7. Talk does not cook rice. (*Chinese*)
8. What one does, one becomes. (*Spanish*)
9. Daylight will peep through a very small hole. (*Japanese*)
10. The creation of a thousand forests is in one acorn. (*American*)

Add your own:

_____

_____

_____

PERSONAL STORIES, MYTHS,
AND DREAMS

Sitting in a group circle, an individual can recount an amusing or harrowing incident, a summer experience, or something that recently happened to a friend or relative. While the story is being told, the rest of the group acts it out in fantasy mime, becoming all the characters, props, and environments in the story.

Another way of evolving a personal story is to throw a small ball to anyone in the group, which is sitting in a circle. The player holding the ball starts the story. After a short while (anywhere from five seconds to half a minute), the ball is passed or thrown to another group member, who continues the story. A player may change or add onto the story in any way he or she wishes. The more fantastic, the better. After this "circle story" is completed, the group can further refine it and act it out in fantasy mime. The wonderful thing about group improvisation is that when the material is self-created, the final product is comprised of the contributions of all the individual members. Thus, there is not only a sharing of ideas and feelings but a deep caring about them.

Myths, legends, and biblical tales are excellent sources of

material for fantasy mime. Ann Halperin and her Dancers' Workshop based on the West Coast enact rituals of birth, life, and death and current myths deifying material success. The Performance Group, under the direction of Richard Schechner, incorporated ritualistic mime in *Dionysius in 69*; and the Polish director Growtowski has based many of his theater pieces on mythology. In my workshops, we have enacted numerous creation myths and biblical stories in fantasy mime. In the myth of Pandora—the first woman—for example, the players' bodies made the mysterious box that Pandora opens, letting out all the evils and plagues (and hope) of the world (see Appendix F). In a theater piece about Jonah, the sailors, the boat, the whale, and the townspeople of Nineveh were created from the bodies of the same cast members, thus showing in action the relation and responsibility to one another of all creatures on earth.

Dreams, in a way, are private myths, another extension of the poetic imagination. Under the careful guidance of an experienced leader, one can relive dreams in fantasy mime, including the enactment of the shadowy elements that were represented in the dream—the people, animals, objects, colors, and moods. You can even act out in fantasy mime the parts of the dream that you have avoided facing. However, any interpretation of a deeply personal dream should be conducted under the guidance of an experienced psychologist. Groups can also act out their hopes, aspirations, and dreams for a better world.

DISCUSS DREAMING
As a basis for sleeping dreams, discuss the following:

For I see now that I am asleep
That I dream when I am awake. . . .
PEDRO DE LA BARCA CALDERON

As a basis of waking dreams of hopes and aspirations, discuss the following:

Some people see things
As they are and ask Why;

I dream of things
That never were, and ask
Why not?
GEORGE BERNARD SHAW

With the group, enact a short sleeping dream of hope, fantasy mime style. You may wish to act out portions of the dream

in slow motion   *in color*
with music   *in shadow*

MAKING MYTHS

1. Act out a Greek or Roman myth in fantasy mime. It can be an explanatory myth that deals with creation and the causes of certain natural phenomena, such as Pandora and the explanation for evil and hope. Or the story you act out can be an exemplary myth that recounts the adventures of gods, heroes, and mortals, whose ways and deeds set an example for living. You may use narration and action mime in creating and enacting your story. In acting Pygmalion, for example, some players can represent the clay that Pygmalion carves piece by piece to reveal Galatea. One player can be the narrator. While enacting the story of Helen Keller, a junior-high school student became the water pump so important in Helen's early life.

2. Act out some of Aesop's Fables in fantasy mime—such as that of the frogs who petitioned Jupiter for a king and received a log instead.

3. Act out myths and tales from Africa (beautiful creation stories!) and China as well as other lands. Make a papier-mâché globe, and color in the country where the legend, myth, or fable originated. Put on a series of myths for a S.H.O.W. (Story Hours Of the World).

Add your own:

_____

_____

_____

We hope you have had fun becoming a variety of fantasy mime objects and environments. Players find it one of the most creative and challenging of all activities. Remarked one player: "We became our environments—the chairs we sit in, the tables we put our food on. We became things we take for granted. These things were explored . . . they were lived . . . how ironic, especially when you consider how we ignore them every day."

PLAYER'S DIARY

1. What was the object you most enjoyed becoming? Why?

2. What was the object you most enjoyed becoming with others ? Why?

3. What was your least favorite object? Why?

4. Do you have a favorite poem that you would enjoy enacting in fantasy mime?

5. Do you have a favorite story, parts of which you would like to enact in fantasy mime?

6. What are some of your favorite foods that you would enjoy enacting in fantasy mime?

7. Can you recall any plays you have seen that use fantasy mime form?

8. What plays or parts of plays would you like to enact in the fantasy mime form?

9. In this chapter, in what ways have you learned to cooperate creatively with your friends and classmates?

10. What have you learned about your body through doing the exercises in this chapter? What is your favorite exercise?

Add your own questions, thoughts, and observations.

Suit the action to the word,
the word to the action.

Shakespeare, *Hamlet*

SONO-MIME 7

Imagine two actors playing a pair of robots. One of the robots—a man—moves slowly toward the other robot—a woman. Resembling a castoff from a late-show Frankenstein movie, his feet clank along while his hands move up and down in choppy slow motion. Like an electric toy being cranked up, the woman puts her hand to her face in breathless expectation. The man begins to "speak" in a measured staccato monotone: "Can—I—have—this—dance?" There is a pause as the woman's arm comes down in a semicircular arc. Slowly, she speaks: "Do—you—waltz?"

In sono-mime, these robots *appear* as though they are speaking. In reality, though, two other players—each assigned to one of the actors pantomiming the robot's movements—are speaking the dialogue or making appropriate bleeps or other sounds.

127

HOW TO PLAY SONO-MIME

Now that you have one example of how it is played, sono-mime can be simply defined as follows:

> *Two players act out a situation in pantomime while two other players on the sidelines vocalize their dialogue and/or sounds.*

The enactment of skits and plays in sono-mime is, of course, not limited to playing robots. Groups have played scenes involving puppets, animals, astrological signs, and people of diverse backgrounds. What makes sono-mime such a challenging theater game is that the situations involving the

Two players pantomime a situation while two others on the sidelines vocalize their sounds or dialogue.
(*Photo by Claudia M. Caruana*)

mixture of sound and action are always improvised within a definite structure.

You can see how the spontaneous response to the unfolding of unexpected situations can develop imagination, concentration, and a high degree of give-and-take. In the process of playing, vocalizers take cues from the players who are performing the action. Players doing the pantomime can also take cues from the vocalizers. This is what makes the game so delightful and challenging: There is no one predictable outcome to a skit, but in every case teamwork and cooperation are necessary for the scene or skit to work. Although this theater game requires a considerable amount of concentration and nimble imagination, high school and college students who have played sono-mime have indicated that it helps greatly to spark creative ensemble acting. Actors have remarked that this specific exercise helps them to pick up cues in general. This is because the speaking player has to be sharp in picking up the pantomime player's action and vice versa.

A student in one workshop commented: "Substituting pantomime when dialogue becomes confusing and cannot be instantly conceived has been such an aid to me to justify situations and relive moods of characterization."

GETTING STARTED

Rather than introducing the concept of sono-mime through lengthy discussion, it is better for the leader to demonstrate how it is played. It is a good idea to play sono-mime after experiencing some creative movement and group pantomime. I find it an excellent technique as a bridge from nonverbal exercises to improvisations using dialogue. It is advisable to start with a simple and familiar situation involving a strong *who*, *what*, and *where*. For example, a manager wants the employee to work overtime on the files in the office, and the employee has to get right home to paint the house before it rains—so the seeds of conflict are established. As you can sense, the situation chosen for sono-mime should include opportunities for lots of movement. The objects can all be mimed; their "visibility" will be part of the viewer's imagination.

As soon as the participants understand how the game is played, groups of four players each can be formed. The groups have about five minutes (*too* much preplanning will kill the spontaneity of the skit) to think of a simple plot structure, including such points as (1) *who* the characters will be, their dominant emotional, physical, and social traits; (2) *what* they want (their goals) in the scene; and (3) *where* the action takes place. Players should also know how the skit will begin and how it will end, even if the course of action changes during the actual playing. During the planning, players must, of course, decide who will do the pantomime and who will do the vocalizing. Planning the skits always involves compromise, cooperation, and a great deal of enjoyable group creativity.

DEVELOPMENT

The potentially broad gestures and exaggerated speaking (and singing) of sono-mime are a natural for musicals, melodrama, and farce. One group of students devised an old-fashioned melodrama. About a dozen players were involved in the skit. First, the players worked out the structure of their play, entitled "The Perils of Pamela." They had fun plotting the typical story, wherein the villain (in this case Norris Nogood) tries to win the hand of the heroine (Pamela Prune) through nefarious means. To make money to pay the mortgage, Pamela is forced to walk the streets, where she is defended by Dudley Doright. In preplanning the show, the players made sure there was a beginning, a middle, an end, a conflict, and a strong dramatic question—in this case, will Pamela be saved from the clutches of Norris? Other characters were added, including a faithful mutt for the Prune family. The Narrator, of course, only pantomimed speaking. Someone on the sidelines played his voice.

The skit was done as mock opera, with much of the action performed in slow motion. Two innovations conceived by the students deserve mention. "Commercial" messages to sell products of the 1890s were also enacted in sono-mime. One of these "breaks" to sell "Tilly's Aromatic Hair Cream" came just as Pamela was about to be done in by the inevitable circular saw. The skit in itself was a gem of a parody, with hilarious

The Patchwork Players act out a melodrama.
(*Photo by Harout Merigan*)

movement and outlandish singing. Another innovation was the pantomiming of a jug band during the wedding of Pamela and Dudley. The motley sounds of the instruments were supplied by additional vocalizers on the sidelines. Thus, more students were able to participate in the fun.

Players who are normally more self-conscious than others open up either as mimes or vocalizers. This is because the players concentrating on the action are not encumbered by the fear of speaking dialogue. The vocalizers, in turn, are not self-conscious about speaking or singing because they are on the sidelines and, thus, psychologically removed from the "spotlight."

STAGING

Staging for sono-mime can range from simple to elaborate. Most groups prefer doing the exercise with the emphasis on the process rather than a finished product—for the benefit of the players themselves rather than for an audience. However, even for the benefit of the players, it is important in this game that—unlike most other improvisational exercises—effective composition and blocking be observed to avoid unnecessary confusion as to who is "speaking." It is best to have only one character move and speak at a time. Overlapping of voices will make the action difficult to follow (unless, of course, some voices must intentionally speak in choral unison).

To clear the stage for proper focus and unity of action, it is a good idea to place the vocalizers off to one side of the stage (or whatever playing space is being utilized). The vocalizers ideally should be in a profile position, so that they can observe the pantomimed action and also be visible to the audience. Whenever a player is offstage or does not have the focus of attention, some convention should be established so that this is made clear to the viewers. For example, the player could face upstage in a three-quarter position or freeze. Before making an entrance, a player should be as unobtrusive as possible. For example, in the melodrama, Dudley Doright squatted down offstage while Norris Nogood was twirling his mustache and demanding Pamela's love. Then, just as Norris advanced toward Pamela, Dudley knocked at the imaginary door of the Prune domicile (the knock was supplied by a vocalizer). Hearing the frenzied cries of Pamela, Dudley pounced onto the scene and started to struggle with Norris while the actress playing Pamela gave the two men the focus by retreating to an upstage corner. When Pamela's dog, Spot, came over to bite Norris, Dudley cleared the stage for this bit of action. Other conventions such as an actor coming downstage to make a melodramatic "aside" were also observed. After playing a number of situations in sono-mime, the importance of clear composition and focus usually becomes clear to the participants. In any case, this theater game is an effective tool for learning some of the rudiments of staging and blocking.

EVALUATION

If a skit does not work out exactly as planned, do not worry; invariably, offshoots and variations will occur during the actual playing. After the skit, a brief discussion can take place regarding the believability and clarity of the characters, plot, dialogue, and sense of the environment. Was there too *much* action? Too *little* action? Were the motivations and behavior of the characters consistent in terms of the story? Could the timing be improved? Was the dialogue believable (even with fantasy characters), clear, and consistent with character and plot? Did the players act and react as an ensemble? After the evaluation, players may wish to switch parts as mimes or vocalizers. They may wish to do another skit altogether. Different combinations of players may be tried as well. Do not forget: Sono-mime is an improvisational theater game; experimentation, trial and error, and revision should be encouraged as much as possible.

USES OF SONO-MIME

IN THEATER

As in most improvisational theater exercises, the uses of sono-mime are varied. In speech, sono-mime is excellent for choral speaking and oral interpretation, combining the spontaneous action of mime and the formal beauty of poetry. In studying the history of theater, we come across the interesting character of Livius Andronicus, who introduced tragedy to Roman audiences in 240 B.C. Livius, a freed Greek slave and tragic actor, gets first credit for playing sono-mime. According to theater historian Vera Mowry Roberts: "Finding that his voice gave out when he attempted to do lines, songs, and dance movement simultaneously, he assigned the voice parts to a speaker who stood at the side of the stage while he, voiceless, pantomimed and danced the part."*

In theater, the game also lends itself to understanding different styles of acting. For example, the majestic sweep of both Greek and Shakespearean drama may be tried with the participants improvising movement and dialogue, using as sources dramatic literature, familiar stories, or their own expe-

---

* Vera Mowry Roberts, *On Stage* (New York: Harper & Row, 1962), p. 59.

rience. While rehearsing a scripted play, actors can learn about the offstage life of the characters they are portraying.

For example, two players can pantomime Willy Loman and Linda of *Death of a Salesman* on their first date while two other actors supply their dialogue. In exploring the inner life of Hamlet, an improvisation can be set up in which Hamlet and Rosencrantz act out their feelings while attending the University of Wittenberg. In history, hypothetical interviews can be set up in sono-mime, such as Frederick Douglass and Abraham Lincoln meeting as young boys. What do they say and do? Unlikely interviews can be set up as well—Abbie Hoffman being interviewed by Socrates, showing appropriate actions; or Sojourner Truth meeting Rosa Parks.

ROLE-PLAYING

In role-playing, players learn to put themselves in the position of another person and defend that position through role reversal. Thus, for example, vocalizer and mime work together to understand a controversial social problem.

Dobbs Ferry High School Drama Club members as vocalizers and mimes working together to understand a social problem.
(*Photo by Jonathan Ishie*)

In one sono-mime skit, a student playing a mother discovered her "daughter" was pregnant. The daughter wanted an abortion. A girl playing the voice of the mother wished that the mother would convince her daughter to have the baby. But, instead, the stereotype was portrayed, with the mother pouncing angrily, her voice screaming "slut!" As the person doing the voice said after the sono-mime: "Unfortunately, it's probably a very true portrait of many mothers whose daughters have found themselves 'in trouble.' If she wanted her daughter to have the baby, she should have supported her with love and not fling insults and bitter words." This led to a discussion in the group concerning legal, moral, and religious attitudes regarding abortion, and the roles were reversed, the mother this time "becoming" the daughter and vice versa. The class found the sono-mime role-playing very enlightening and a good opportunity for exchanging points of view.

Other examples of sono-mime role-playing situations and characters include:

1. Conflict between parents and offspring (a family at dinner).
2. Futurism: a dialogue mime between two satisfied/dissatisfied (pick one) robots. (The dissatisfied robots will spark a more *interesting* conflict.)
3. Argument between husband and wife over a task that has to be done in the home.
4. Someone has taken something that belongs to another person in the group.
5. A person in his or her middle fifties who has just lost a job is trying to get a new one.
6. An eighteen-year-old woman trying to convince her father to approve of her desire to move out.

Many of the uses of sono-mime can be combined in a unified learning experience. For example, one group recreated the assassination of Abraham Lincoln in sono-mime. Lincoln and his wife were interviewed at the Ford's Theater using a "You Are There" format. In the meantime, onstage other players were watching *Our American Cousin*. The broad and humorous actions of the melodrama contrasted chillingly with the startling turn of events signaled by Booth's sudden appearance. Through this exercise, the players internalized a meaningful historical event, learned about nineteenth-century American theater, and experienced the collective creation of putting together a theatrical–historical "happening."

When the improvisational and planned elements of sono-mime merge as one, reflected in the spontaneous interplay of pantomime and speech, the feeling of good ensemble work is greatly evidenced. As a means to enhance group playing or as a creative end in itself, you will find sono-mime a challenging theater activity.

PLAYER'S DIARY

1. Which part did you enjoy playing most—the speaker or the mime?

2. Which situations were the easiest to enact? The hardest?

3. Can you think of other situations you would like to enact?

4. What did you learn about cooperation while doing this exercise?

5. What else did you learn from doing this exercise?

Add your own questions, thoughts, and observations.

All things must change
To something new,
to something strange

Longfellow

TRANSFORMATIONS 8

The heart of the creative process is transformation—going through creative changes. We start with an idea or image, a feeling or impulse—some kind of impression based on inner experience. Then we try to give expression to this impression by shaping it through a process of trial and error, elaborated insight, and revision. The process of transformation helps to ignite the creative spark in every one of us.

In previous work described in this book, you have isolated the senses for greater body awareness. Transformation exercises allow for the integration of all the senses, including the sixth sense—intuition—so that mind and body are working as one in the creation of improvisational situations. Just as sensory work strengthens concentration, so transformation exercises further stretch imagination. In the process of moving quickly and spontaneously from one image to another, give-and-take within an ensemble is sharpened. Group transformations enable actors to adjust quickly to changing characters, conditions, and circumstances.

137

THE CONCEPT

The concept of transformation in this country was originated by Viola Spolin when she served as workshop director of the Second City Company in Chicago. Joe Chaikin, who also worked with Second City, brought the transformation concept back to New York in the 1960s and developed it in the Open Theatre, which he founded. As an example of the Open Theatre's work, in *Viet Rock* the actors created the jungle terrain with their bodies. With their voices, they simultaneously created the sounds of the raging battle. An American soldier would mime being shot while others caught the falling body. The sounds sharply underwent change to orchestrate this action, and then the body was lifted high into the air. The ensemble made weird contrapuntal sounds as they transformed themselves into a twirling helicopter, which transported the wounded soldier to Saigon. Seconds later, with only their bodies and appropriate sounds comprising the stage reality, the ensemble became the structures and fixtures of a Saigon hospital; seconds later, these were transformed into a Buddhist funeral.

The beautiful thing about fantasy mime transformations is that you can create an entire stage reality with a small cast. The very style of production with a cast of four or five demands that the actors and director find imaginative ways to shift from one scene or moment to the next. The Pantomime Circus, directed by Lotte Goslar, performs an interesting sequence called "Circus Scene" in which a four-part lion separates to become a pack of wolves after their prey. Half of the Patchwork Players (consisting of seven players) created the atmospheres and environments of the Land of Honah Lee, and the other half of the company transformed themselves into Puff, the Magic Dragon. During the verses, half of the company (who, minutes before, were the environments of trees, rocks, and so forth) transformed themselves into the boat with billowed sails where Jackie Paper keeps his lookout, perched on Puff's tail. Seconds later, the boat broke up to become the characters of noble kings and princes who bow before Puff. Instead of Jackie Paper giving Puff real or imaginary string, it

A lion resting before its death at the hands of the clown. From *Circus Scene,* after a scenario by Bertolt Brecht for Lotte Goslar's Pantomime Circus.

(Photo by John Lindquist, courtesy of Lotte Goslar)

Jackie Paper embraces Puff the Magic Dragon in a scene performed by the Patchwork Players.

(Photo by Alex Gersznowicz)

was made from two or three bodies floating in space. Seconds later, the noble characters once again transformed themselves into the trees, rocks, and bushes of Honah Lee during the chorus; finally, they became the cave for Puff to step into.

JUST FOR STARTERS

As warm-ups, pass one sound around a circle, and then transform it the second time around into another sound (see Chapter 3). Then pass around one face (based upon a specific inner life), stretching the muscles like a mask; transform the face as it goes around the circle. Last, add one sound and one face, and transform them both. These exercises develop spontaneity. After first doing this transformation sitting down, the group can stand in place and continue the exercise, using their whole bodies.

SOUND-AND-MOTION TRANSFORMATIONS

1. After some loosening up exercises, such as jumping in place, dangling and shaking arms and feet, touching toes, playing an imaginary piano, the group is ready.

2. Two lines facing each other are formed. A player initiates a movement in place and adds a sound flowing out of this movement. The player crosses over to the other side of the room and passes the movement and sound to another player. It is important that the two players occupy the same kinetic space for a bit, getting in touch with each other, so that Player B can synchronously catch Player A's movement.

3. Player B, after imitating A's sound and movement, slowly transforms it so that, in effect, he or she is now initiating a new movement that has grown out of the first movement and sound. Player B then crosses to the other side. This exercise is very liberating for players once they get the knack of it.

HOT AND COLD

This exercise helps you to use your imagination while exploring the relationship between opposites.

1. Two groups form two lines facing each other with plenty of space in between. The leader calls out two contrasting or opposing words. These words can be nouns or adjectives: *hot* and *cold; bitter* and *sweet; tall* and *short; old* and *young; vinegar* and *perfume; reality* and *fantasy; light* and *heavy; football* and *baseball;* and so on.

2. As a set of words is called out, a player from each side moves toward the center line, each player interpreting through sound and movement one of the words the leader has called out. At the center line, the two players exchange each other's exact movements and sounds. Thus, for two players interpreting *old* and *young,* an old man is suddenly transformed into a bouncy baby, and the bouncy baby becomes the old man. Sometimes two opposites meeting can transform into a substance or form that is a synthesis of the two words. Thus, *old* and *young* become something halfway in between. The exercise can be played in exaggerated slow time or extra fast.

It is a good exercise to understand quickly changing emotions, as in Scene 4 of *Romeo and Juliet,* when both characters suffer the extremes of happiness and sorrow, realizing their deep love for each other and discovering they are parts of enemy houses.

CREATE-A-WORLD

1. One person goes into the center of the circle and creates the essence of an activity through movement and pantomime. Say it is the world of sports. The player might be running on a tennis court, for example.

2. After thirty seconds or so of this activity, Player 2 enters the circle and joins the first person's world. Player 2, for example, could play tennis with Player 1 or play a different sport entirely.

3. After another fifteen seconds or so, Player 2 changes the world into anything he or she wants—say, the world of musical instruments. In any case, there should be marked contrast, both in idea and movement, to the preceding world.

4. Player 1 now joins the newly created world.

5. Then Player 3 joins the world of the first two players, and after a while, he or she changes it into another world, which is

Create-a-world with the On-the-Spot Players, directed by Milton Polsky. The young woman in the middle is about to change the world of sports into the world of music.
(Photo by Leonard Lewis)

joined by the first two players. This process is continued until everyone is in the circle, creating marvelous worlds of reality and fantasy—the worlds of work, circuses, sports, leisure, friendship, strife, etc.

One high-school director, Barbara Endleman, in her work with *Raisin in the Sun,* had the cast familiarize themselves with the different locales of the Younger household through a variation called "Create-a-Scene." For example, the player portraying Travis created one of the numerous bald spots in the living room rug, and Ruth and Walter created the essence of banging continually on the imaginary bathroom door, a part of the household constantly frustrating all the characters. Each player obtained a good sense of the small space available in the house and the essence of the residents coming into conflict with each other.

In social studies or history, many worlds can be created—for example, in the black experience, the horrors of slavery being transmitted through words and movement, then transforming that world into the world of resistance to slavery, into

Create a world of space fantasy.
(Photo by Archaesus Productions, 1975. Gary Young, Producing Director)

the world of civil rights, and so on. In science classes, players can create the worlds of the nervous or circulatory systems, or of cells and atoms, and so forth.

THE MAGIC SCARF

This is a good exercise for transforming real objects into other things and then associating a character and action with the object. I believe it was John Dewey who wrote that art is the celebration of the ordinary. The scarf serves as a trigger to release the magic *inside* you, so that you can become anybody you want, anywhere, anytime.

1. Make a large circle. An ordinary scarf is thrown to someone in the group. The player turns the scarf into anything the imagination will allow. Go right to it, making a sleeping baby, a slithering snake, a bullfighter's cape, or what have you.

2. After everyone has had a solo turn, the exercise continues with a player transforming the scarf, getting into character, and then spontaneously relating to one other person. For example, if a player changes the scarf into a dog leash, another player may become the dog or a dogcatcher. When working in

What kinds of things and characters can the Magic Scarf suggest?

(Photos by P. A. Munch and Harout Merigan)

pairs, the first player should think of a goal and make it physical, and the other person can become the obstacle blocking the attainment of the goal. This is a delightful exercise for young and old. As one player in a workshop said: "I couldn't believe how many objects that grubby scarf could become. . . . I guess it has more important things to do than sit in one's hair . . . we used it for a veil for a bride, then as a noose, a snake charmer, and a matador's cape, and I became a bull—I don't do that every day."

ACTIVITY-FANTASY MIME:
TRANSFORMATION FROM STORIES AND THEATER

1. The Wizard of Oz turns himself into an eccentric elephant, lady in green, ball of fire, etc.
2. The Evil Magician, von Rothbart, puts a spell on young girls and turns them into swans (Swan Lake).
3. Wizard turns prince into frog.
4. Dr. Jekyll transforms into Mr. Hyde.
5. Alice shrinking (and becoming larger than life).

In the Manhattan Theatre Project (directed by Andre Gregory) version of Alice in Wonderland, arched backs formed wickets, and scrunched-up bodies became deliciously funny croquet balls during the Queen of Hearts' game of croquet. Fantasy scenes featured human mushrooms and a "bread-stuffed" dormouse as integral parts of the show.

CRAZY Xs

In teams of three, make the following transformations in fantasy mime:

1. What do you get when you cross a porcupine with a sheep? (A creature that knits its own sweaters.)
2. What do you get when you cross a turtle with a cow? (A turtleneck jersey.)
3. What do you get when you cross jelly and water? (Ocean currents.)

Crazy Xs—guess of what.

(*Photos courtesy of Archaesus Productions, 1975, Gary Young, Producing Director and by Jonathan Ishie*)

4. What do you get when you cross a book and a worm? (A bookworm.)

5. Make up your own crazy Xs!

FANTASY TRUNK

A fantasy guide is selected, who outlines the dimensions of an invisible trunk. The class surrounds the trunk chanting, "Fantasy Trunk, Fantasy Trunk, trick or treat, but not some junk!" Six players enter the circle and, one at a time, extract imaginary objects of their choice from the trunk. The fantasy guide (leader) and the rest of the class ask each player questions about his or her object. The players then *transform themselves into their objects.* The rest of the class breaks up into smaller groups and makes up a story incorporating all six objects. A storyteller in each group then tells the tale involving the six resting objects, who come alive as soon as they are mentioned during the unfolding of the story.

TIME TO TRANSFORM

The origins of drama are found in magical fertility rites, half-danced and half-mimed, which were an attempt to control supernatural forces related to survival. If hunting tribes lacked meat, they would enact a hunting scene, some men impersonating the game and others, the successful party of hunters. The first dramas depicted the conflict between life and death. If a hero or god of the tribe was portrayed as slain, it was imperative that he be resurrected as well; thus, he might represent the death of winter and the renewal of spring and summer. He might be the spirit of corn or other symbols of the harvest. People would mimic a rainstorm in the hope of getting one and transform themselves into animals and food during the process of imitative magic. In a way, transformation is magic, and participants can learn a great deal about drama and the basic conflicts of life through enacting ancient rituals.

Transformations can be enacted to help students to become aware of and experience life cycles; humankind's basic needs; the vital functions of animals, plants, and other things in the scheme of reproduction and evolution—an amoeba ingesting and dividing; unborn birds breaking out of shells; flowers going to seed. How are the basic needs of human life similar to those of a tree? In which ways are all basic needs of life similar? What are some of the differences in the ways a human takes in food and the way an amoeba takes in food? How do the seasons and weather conditions affect life?

INDIVIDUAL SITUATIONS

1. While walking through the forest, you find a magic Golden Frisbee. Slowly become this frisbee and change into another flying object.
2. Become a piece of driftwood as it is washed up on the shore.
3. You are a piece of thread dangling from a needle. Sew something.
4. You are a dinasour egg. Grow into a giant "whatever," and have someone ride on top of you.
5. You are a tall building tumbling down. Show through movement and sound how you feel.
6. While walking through an apartment, you are transformed into a chair. Show us how you would feel if different people were to sit on you or the chair tumbled over.

SITUATIONS FOR TWO OR THREE PLAYERS

1. You and your partner are climbing a magic mountain. When you get to the top, slowly transform into what you see in the valley below.
2. You and your companions are strange undersea creatures caught in a giant whirlpool. Slowly mirror each other, and merge into one.
3. You and your companions are attempting to cross a busy intersection. When you get halfway across the street, become a car or bus, and try to dodge the jaywalkers.

4. You and your partner are playing a duet on a piano. You become the piano keys, and have your partner play on you. (Substitute any instruments of the orchestra, and make a human symphony.) Becoming musical instruments is especially fun. Remarked one student: "She sat down and played the piano keys—me. I moved up and down when pressed and released. Although I was just a note, I felt like I had a personality. When my note was touched, I emitted a loud, off-key 'so,' then moved my body the way I thought an off-key 'so' would move."

5. You are children in your playroom. You slowly transform into your favorite toys. Show how you would act in a deserted, haunted house.

SITUATIONS FOR GROUPS
(FIVE TO TEN PEOPLE)

1. You and your friends are transformed into microbes by a solar ray. Through movement and sound, show your various shapes and forms.

2. You are a party of fishermen. Transform several members of the group into seaweed trying to untangle itself from a hook on a fishing line.

3. While digging for artifacts, your group of archaeologists find some prehistoric bones. Construct a giant dinosaur using the bodies of some members of the group. (Even though the dinosaurs are dead, as the bones are constructed the addition of sounds will make the skit more theatrically effective.)

4. While exploring an ancient and musty cave, your team of archaeologists spot a prehistoric ant colony. The team transforms into this giant colony and prepares its defenses at the sound of human footsteps.

5. Surveying an uncharted planet, your exploring party is suddenly transformed into strange antibodies that devour all life forms.

6. You are scuba divers exploring ancient treasure. Become this treasure.

7. A space team is transformed into a giant news computer. Give your planet's latest news flash.

8. The team is transformed into the animals and plants of a solar space-park.

9. One-half of the team becomes a forest and the other half, pollutants that threaten the safety of the forest.

10. Your party is enjoying a meal in a restaurant. Transform into the kitchen, and become the food you are eating.

11. Your group is capsizing on a small raft. Become the raft, passengers, and tidal wave.

12. The group comes upon an uncharted body of water. You are suddenly transformed into a giant terrestrial squid.

13. Half the group becomes a stream, and the rest of the group becomes the particles that pollute it.

14. Through sound and movement, create a massive intergalactic universe revolving in space.

15. You are a group of lumberjacks chopping down a forest. Two or three stubborn trees won't fall. Show what happens.

A NOTE ON PREPARING SITUATIONS

In preparing transformations, keep them as open-ended as possible, so that the players can resolve the problem using their own imaginative alternatives. Keep the situations dramatic with a built-in conflict, and keep them *brief*. The following is an example of an *ineffectual* situation as written: "You and your friend are walking on a crowded street. A tourist bus drives by and stops for a red light. You observe a person throwing paper (which your friend has transformed into) from the bus. Admonish the bus passenger for being a polluter." There is simply too much happening here; and, more importantly, the situation tells how the conflict should be resolved, making it closed-ended. Better: "You and your friend are walking down a clean street when a third person throws down some paper (which your friend transforms into). What do you do?"

Here are some transformational situations created by students in my Summer Institute of Drama for Teachers:

1. You and your partner are lost in a desert when one of you is transformed into the North Star. Show how you would guide the other.

2. You are transformed into the first group of monkeys on Mars. Show how you would explore the planet.

3. You are in a desert when your shadow (another player) transforms you into a threatening being. What do you do?

4. You are teaching your child to swim when he or she turns into a fish. What do you do?

5. You are visualizing a tree, watching its changes through the seasons, when you are slowly transformed into the tree during the various seasons. Show these changes through your body and sounds.

Add your own:

_____

_____

_____

ADVANCED WORK

Advanced work in transformations can be made more interesting through basic tumbling techniques such as head stands, somersaults, cartwheels, and forward rolls. For example, the enactment of "Four and Twenty Blackbirds" might go something like this:

TEXT	ACTION
Sing a song of sixpence *Pocketful of rye*	Cast of six players lines up in a straight line, sings first two lines, miming taking a nip from a bottle in each of their pockets.

TEXT	ACTION
Four and twenty blackbirds *Baked in a pie.*	Players cartwheel into birds, fly around. Three players break off, become round pie. Other three players do forward rolls, landing in pie.
When the pie was opened, *The birds began to sing;* *Wasn't that a tasty dish* *To set before the king?*	The pie-players do back-bends; birds fly around singing. One pie-player becomes a throne; another player becomes king and sits on the throne.
The king was in the count-ing house *Counting out his money* *The queen was in the parlor* *Eating bread and honey.*	Third pie-player becomes scale. On other side of stage, one bird transforms into queen; another bird does tiger leap and trans-forms into table. Third bird cartwheels, transforming into a maid serving queen from table.
The maid was in the garden *Hanging out the clothes* *Along came a blackbird and snipped off her nose.*	Maid does a forward roll to other side of stage. King and throne do backward rolls, straighten up and be-come clothesline. Scale and table do shoulder stands and become wet clothes that maid hangs up. Queen is transformed into black-bird that snips off maid's nose.

A number of basic gymnastic and yoga techniques can be applied to fantasy mime transformations: Cobra, Fish Flop, No Hands Roll, Shoulder Stands, Tiger Leap, and Yoga Head-stands. It should be pointed out that most people are capable of doing all these physical exercises—even the most difficult ones. It is not a matter of strength or even of great skill. It is simply that some bodies are not quite ready to do the exercises; are not relaxed enough to allow their muscles to go far enough. When the time is right—with practice and confidence in one's capabilities—almost everyone can do each exercise without overtaxing effort.

TRANSFORMATIONS WITH YOUNG PEOPLE

When young people *experience* the content they are learning in class, factual information becomes more permanently fixed in their minds, because the subject matter has been internalized during the process of undergoing emotional changes. Thus, while becoming the parts of a ship (wheels, rudders, sails, mast), students learn that the wind blows the sails attached by lines to the mast, and that the wheel steers the ship via its rudder, which is located at the back of the ship. By moving their bodies, the players discover that in order to turn the ship portside (left), they have to turn the wheel starboard (right). If children and/or teenagers are studying about forest fire prevention, they can first be riding through the country.

Students studying ships become the parts of one to understand the subject better. (*Photo by Bob Cannistraci*)

They themselves can become the fire and the wind blowing flames across the grass. Other students can put out the fire, and a discussion can be held about different ways to prevent fires. The young people, in effect, have become their own lesson. In the process of cooperating to put on the skit, the group becomes the subject matter as well.

One fifth-grade teacher effectively combined drama and dance with her students to study ecology. Several students formed a large rock. Others became wind, rain, and sun acting upon the rock until it broke up into little pieces small enough for a plant's root to absorb. What happens to a rock after the environment works on it? It changes into what? What experiences do both living and nonliving things undergo?

TRANSFORMATION CYCLES: TWO TREES

Two groups are formed. Group 1 works on the following transformations (suggested, in part, by Janet McClelland):

Tree → paper → box → paperdoll → letter → envelope → advertising poster → things drawn on poster → paper airplane → paper bag → book → paper flower → tree → ?

Group 2 also starts with a tree. Possibilities:

Tree → log → board → chair → table → wooden doll → soldier → telephone pole → ladder → sliver of wood → tree → ?

Group 3:

solid mass → liquid → gas → ?

Complete the following transformations, so that (in the words of Leonard Bernstein) "this becomes that."

- Rope →
- Rain →
- Snow →
- Sand →
- Fire →

FANTASY MIME FOOD

1. Start with a raw egg, and slowly transform into a beaten egg⟶ a fried egg⟶ a scrambled egg⟶ an omelete.

2. Start with a seed, and slowly transform into beans⟶ rice⟶ patties⟶ cake⟶ cake with candles⟶ melting candles⟶ wax⟶ wax flowers⟶ flour⟶ bread⟶ seeds⟶

3. Start with a cow, and slowly transform into milk⟶milk shake⟶ float⟶ sundae⟶ nuts⟶ (Yes, you are, to see how far this can go!)

4. Give character traits to foods:

- "Slippery" banana
- "Sniffly" grapefruit
- "Tough" carrots
- "Spongy" batter
- "Lush" tomato

Add your own:

_____

_____

_____

In summary, transformation is metamorphosis and magic. It is a cocoon blooming into a butterfly, a tree turning into a book, with all the characters coming alive. It is rain becoming an ocean, soaking up the salt from rocks, and evaporating into snowflakes falling, making a blanket on the ground, and then turning into a snowball, into a snowman, into an igloo, then melting to the ground. Acts of transformation are the strands of creativity. Transformation and fantasy mime are work and play tied together in so many ways.

SEQUENCE I

This sequence illustrates the marvelous creativity that can result when you mix fantasy mime and transformation.

WARM-UP: MAGIC MOVER

For five minutes or so, play Magic Mover (Chapter 1) with the whole group.

TRANSFORMATION: MAGIC SCARF

In groups of no more than six players, transform your scarves (Chapter 8) into objects; become characters associated with them; and develop conflicts and resolutions.

SKIT: MAGIC

This new exercise must be experienced to be believed. "Magic's" charm and power derive from its very simplicity.

1. Circle formation. Quickly go around the circle as each player volunteers a word or two regarding what the word *magic* suggests.
2. Break up into groups of four or five each.
3. In no more than ten minutes, each group prepares a skit that involves, at one time or another, some sort of magic in it. The "magic" is by no means limited to the kind associated with hats and rabbits; in fact, the suggestions offered in step 1 will effectively trigger the imaginations.
4. Enjoy the skits. (No examples are offered at this time, so that your own wonderful products will be completely original and totally surprising.)

SEQUENCE 2

Here is a sequence outlining an effective *progression* of transformational activity:

WARM-UP

1. Pass around same sound and then transform (*seated*).
2. Pass around same face and then transform (*seated*).
3. Pass around same face *and* sound and then transform (*seated*).
4. Sound-motion transformation (*moving*).

DEVELOPMENT

1. Hot and Cold (*in pairs, moving*).
2. Create-a-World (*action and fantasy mime, moving*).
3. Feedback-kinds of worlds created.

CULMINATION

1. Circle story (*group*).
2. Gibberish (*groups and pairs*).
3. Gibberviews (*skits in 3s*).
4. Feedback and discussion: focus on two aspects of awareness, on values of concentration, imagination, and cooperation and on drama values—expressiveness, conflict, and characterization.

PLAYER'S DIARY

1. What is your favorite poem—one that you would like to do someday in fantasy mime transformation?
2. Do you have a favorite story that you would like to do in transformation?
3. How did it feel to play "Create-a-World"? Could you write a poem or make a collage about the experience?
4. Describe what "transformation" is in your own words.
5. What have you learned about your body and imagination through the exercises in this chapter?

Add your own questions, thoughts, and observations.

CHARACTERS IN CONFLICT 9

The basic element of drama—the confrontation of two characters who want to do something with each other, for each other, or to each other—is explored in the following two exercises.

TWISTS AND TURNS

Virtually everyone who has played Twists and Turns loves it. A primary value of the exercise is that it develops highly imaginative responses to all sorts of unexpected turns of events as actors play off one another. It builds spontaneity and concentration as a player stays in character and reacts to another character. Players learn to carry out a dramatic confrontation, not merely a conversation.

1. All the players are seated on the floor in circle formation. Do some mirrors as a warm-up for a few minutes.

2. Two players, designated 1 and 2, twist and turn around for no more than five seconds.

3. The leader says "freeze," and the two players stop their twisting action.

4. Player 1 finds a physical attitude suggested in Player 2's body position. For example, say Player 2's hands are spread apart in an open position, palms up, showing great weight and strain. His face is grimacing, and his knees are slightly bent. He might be carrying a basin of hot water.

5. Player 1 enters the situation, adding the element of conflict. For example, she might be Player 2's mother, trying to help him carry the basin of hot water into the house. But Player 2, to extend the conflict, wants to carry the basin alone. Thus, Player 2 could be a young boy. The conflict develops, with each player portraying why the boy should or should not carry the basin in alone.

At all times, the players should be aware of (1) *who* they

"Be careful with that basin of water!"
(*Photo by Jonathan Ishie*)

"What marvelous fabric! Where can I buy some?"
(*Photo by Jonathan Ishie*)

are (and should show this by at least one dominant physical characteristic); (2) *what* they want in the scene—that is, their goal; and (3) *where* they are. For example, the boy wants to do the job alone; the mother wants to help him. They could be in the backyard. The mother could be hanging wash on the clothesline; seeing her son, she goes over to help him. The boy might decide not to bring in the basin but to play basketball instead as the resolution of the conflict.

6. After a minute or so of establishing, developing, and resolving the conflict, Player 1 sits down; and a new participant, Player 3, spins around with Player 2, and a new conflict with new characters is developed. The exercise continues until everyone in the circle has had an opportunity to participate.

7. Discuss the kinds of roles that developed during the improvisations.

DEVELOPMENT

After everyone has had a chance to experience the game at least once, take it one step further by making the game even more challenging. Try playing it with different acting styles and play forms. As before, two players spin around. Freeze. Player A "takes it off" B. This time, though, do it as though you were in a Greek or Shakespearean tragedy with lofty poetic dialogue and stylized gestures. Go! Freeze! Reverse. B takes it off A. Do it as a TV soap opera (capture the essence: lots and lots of exposition, morbid melodrama, repetition of names, and so forth). For example, the earlier dialogue with the boy and his mom might now go like this.

> MOM: *"Bob, I heard from Nurse Smith, who heard it from Doctor Brown, who heard it on his radio coming in from Soaptown after visiting his arthritic sister Agnes, the one who's in love with that young upstart lawyer, who just moved in from New York after a scandal involving his daughter Carol, that your back is sprained, so you can't carry the basin by yourself!"*
>
> BOB: *"I want to carry the basin, Mom. I want to do it for Carol!"*
>
> MOM: *"You mean, you know Carol!?"*
>
> BOB: *"Yes, Mom—her clothes are in here!"*

Other variations in styles include:

- TV game show: lots of jerky movement, forced frivolity, hokey suspense
- 1930s musicals: Boy meets girl, loses girl, finds girl; players can sing and dance
- Mystery show: action, intrigue, staccato dialogue, cafés, and half-lit corners
- Hospital show: interns and nurses, danger, rescues, and daring operations
- "Sesame Street": animals, letters, puppets, singing, and dancing
- Commercials of all kinds
- Robots and monsters
- Gibberish
- Slow motion

- Pinter, Ibsen, Williams situations and dialogue
- Characters in the play you are rehearsing.

VARIATIONS

1. *Three* players twist and turn. One player is instructed to "take it off" another player; after fifteen seconds or so, the third player joins the conflict, either taking sides with one of the players or adding a different sort of complication. For example, two players argue about where a picture should be placed on a wall. The third player is from an art gallery, reclaiming the picture; the first two players join forces.

A three-person conflict by the Proposition Circus, directed by Allan Albert.
(*Photo courtesy of Allan Albert*)

2. "As the World Twists and Turns"—soap opera or good old-fashioned melodrama. Start off with two players; then keep adding more, one every twenty or thirty seconds. When a new name is mentioned in dialogue, that person can materialize.

HE: *It's true? Margaret was seen with young Dr. Malone?*
SHE: *More than once!*

DR. MALONE (entering in huff): *Margaret, I won't have my love slandered. You're no worse than that new upstart lawyer, Henry Backscratch.*
HE: *Look—he's coming.*
SHE: *That pest . . .*
BACKSCRATCH (entering): *Where's Malone—that ingrate!*

AUDIENCE INVOLVEMENT

1. The rest of the players who are "audience" can, when appropriate, make accompanying sounds during a Twist and Turn enactment: "canned" laughter during a sitcom, organ music for a "soap," applause for singing and dancing players.

2. The entire cast Twists and Turns. Freeze! Audience calls out a place, for example, cocktail party. Each player then unfreezes for a second, and utters a word or phrase flowing out of his or her "statue" position. A sort of "ripple effect" of words can take place before starting a new group Twist and Turn.

Twists and Turns and audience involvement. On-the-Spot Player elicits suggestions from the audience as to when the improvisation should take place—the past, present, or future. The girl holding the trunk will become Cleopatra moving her belongings down the Nile.

(Photo by Leonard Lewis)

CHARACTERS IN CONFLICT

3. Just before a Twist and Turn duo are unfrozen, the audience can be asked to supply a "frame" for the improv to occupy. Examples of such frames include the following:

- home, school, work
- past, present, future
- city, country, suburbia.

Add your own:

_____   _____

_____   _____

_____   _____

POINTERS FOR PLAYERS

1. When starting the improv, focus on an outstanding physical attribute of the opposite player—literally something that stands out, whether it be a crooked finger, a raised elbow, a

When the player on the right unfreezes, he will question the other player who spotted the $50 bill first.
(Photo by Mary Alfieri)

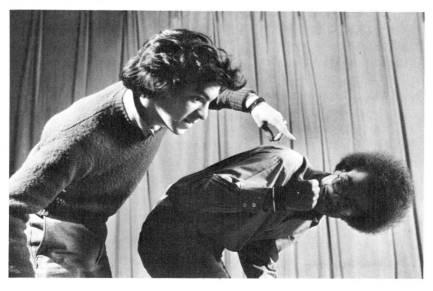

tilted head, or the like. As soon as you have singled out and seized upon the physical characteristic, start dialoguing. There is the danger of thinking too much at the initial stage. To get the game rolling, follow and act upon your impulses.

2. Keep the energy level flowing. Be mindful of the other person's objectives as they develop. If one goal dominates, be prepared to give the scenic moment to the other player. Stay in character at all times. Don't use real names. Make up character names on the spot: Mom, Sis, Dr. Smith, Mabel, and so forth. Ask yourself what you want from the other character and how you will go about getting it. Be aware of the newly created environment as an important element of the improvisation.

3. Play for scenic truth; acting is larger than life, but communicate the basic truth of the character as you feel it. Personal and group awareness is deepened when the learning experience is a pleasurable one. This exercise is no exception. Have fun!

MISSIONS POSSIBLE

In a sense, all actors and actresses have an important mission—to convince an audience that real things are happening to real people. Where most beginning actors fail to communicate is in believably portraying the goals of their characters. In order to perform any role effectively, players must constantly be aware of the *who, what,* and *where.*

The "Missions Possible" exercise is designed precisely to help the actor learn to play spontaneous situations with a sense of truth and urgency. The structure of the exercise is provided through the actor's "given circumstances"—the three Ws. Let's continue with a description and an example of how the exercise is performed.

The room is dark. Suddenly a flashlight is flicked on. The light's beam focuses on a tape recorder in the center of the room. The machine is switched on, and we hear a voice slowly and carefully transmit the following instructions:

"Attention all agents! You are about to receive your Mission Possible!
(*Photo by Jonathan Ishie*)

The leader should make sure the *where* is not included on the Missions Possible slip
... the *where* is chosen by the group as a whole.
(*Photo by Jonathan Ishie*)

Attention all agents! Attention all agents! You are about to receive your "Missions Possible." While playing your situations, at all times it is important to remember three things: (1) who you are, (2) what your goal is, and (3) where you are. Repeat: who, what, where. This tape will self-destruct in five seconds. Good luck!

1. After the tape is heard, sealed envelopes (with the word *secret* printed on them) are passed around to all the participants. Each player opens an envelope to find a slip of paper with a situation written on it. On each slip of paper is written a character (*who*) and his or her goal (*what*).

Some examples:

- You are an *escaped convict* who must find a place to hide.
- You are a *teacher* on vacation who wants peace and quiet.
- You are a famous *heart surgeon* rushing to save the life of a transplant patient.
- You are a *gossip columnist* looking for a juicy story.
- You are an *expectant mother/father* who must get to the hospital.
- You are a *conservationist* trying to save a species in danger of extinction.
- You are a *novelist* racing to meet a deadline on your new book.
- You are an *ecology "freak"* who sees pollution everywhere.

Add your own:

_____

_____

_____

Do not reveal the contents of the envelopes to anyone.

2. Two volunteers are asked to play the first improvisation. The leader takes the envelopes and asks the two players—let's say, Alice and Burt—to leave the room. While waiting outside, they are not to discuss the information on their slips of paper.

3. With Alice and Burt out of the room, the rest of the group is told what the two situations are. Let's say Alice's slip says she's the famous novelist who must meet a book deadline. Burt is the eco-freak who looks for signs of pollution wherever he goes. The group as a whole now decides on the *where*, which must be a logical, natural place where *both* characters could be. After considering the deck of a ship, a deserted office building, the zoo at Central Park, and other locales, the group decides on a secluded beach.

4. After the *where* has been chosen, Alice and Burt return to the room and are both informed that their actions take place on a beach. The leader may now briefly edit or enlarge upon

The novelist trying to get rid of the eco-freak, who draws back in horror from her "pollution."
(*Photo by Jonathan Ishie*)

the *where* to clarify and facilitate playing. For example: It's early morning, the tide has come in, there's a table with a few chairs in front of a beach house, there's a typewriter on top of the table, the wind is blowing, and so forth.

5. At this time, the leader may also wish to clarify *briefly* for each player the *who* and *what*. For example, the leader may whisper to Alice that she has to mail her manuscript in fifteen minutes and needs absolute peace and quiet to finish and will tolerate *no* interruptions. Burt, the eco-freak, is privately told by the leader that he cannot stand the sight of even the slightest piece of paper being thrown on the ground.

6. Before starting the improvisation, Burt and Alice close their eyes and in their own minds consider, first of all, how they happen to be *where* they are now. *What* did they come here to do? What will they be doing just prior to the moment when the improv begins? What are other stimuli affecting their choice of action—the temperature, the time of day, the surrounding objects? *Who* are they? How old? Is there one particular speech trait or physical gesture that may help to define the characters?

The novelist insists: "I've got five minutes to finish this last page. Get out of here!" (*Photo by Jonathan Ishie*)

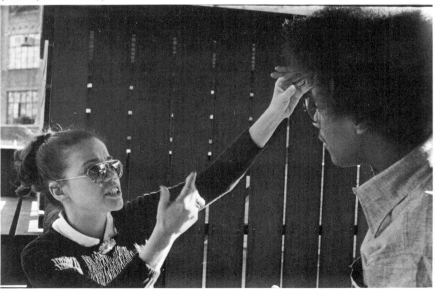

7. The players perform for about four or five minutes without interruption—except for occasional brief coaching, such as the leader reminding them to focus on their goals. It is important that during the improv, players reveal who they are only through what they say and do. For example, Alice should not say to Burt: "Don't bug me, I'm an important novelist, and I have to finish this book." Instead, she must *show* she is a novelist through working on her book, talking about it, or through other appropriate words and actions. Burt does not directly announce, "I'm an eco-freak," but *shows* he is one through his dialogue and actions.

8. Each improv is followed by brief comments. Was the improv believable? Why? Why not? Were the actors playing their goals? What was the relationship of one character to the other? What did they want from each other as the situation developed? Were the actions clear?

VALUES

The actors learn to think on their feet within a given situation and structural framework. Concentration is developed as the players focus on their goals. Powers of observation are sharpened as they utilize the five senses while interacting with the imagined physical environment. Their imagination is stimulated as they create their own dialogue and body responses. They learn to trust their own intuitions and gut feelings while creating a character.

The player also becomes aware of the other actor's contribution in the scene. A large part of acting is reacting—reacting not in a predetermined, stereotyped fashion but in a fresh, honest way as the improvisation proceeds from moment to moment. Sometimes the player's major goal must be adjusted as he or she spontaneously reacts to the unfolding of unexpected developments caused by a twist in plot or change of mood. A strong goal incites character to action, and changing moods shape the meaning even deeper. In short, the actor learns to deal with conflict—the heart of drama—and complications—the life-blood of drama. Through actively learning the dynamics of drama, the player can better appreciate the nature of theater and the creative problems of the theater artist.

The immediate lesson is that when two people playing opposite each other have strong goals, sparks begin, or should begin, to ignite. If they fail to catch on, it is either because the actors are not playing their goals strongly enough or because strong goals are not there to begin with. In an improvisation, either possibility can occur. This, too, can serve as a valuable basis for discussion.

Because the two actors do not overtly know who the other is and must rely on a trading of emotional relationships rather than merely of information, usually the characterizations created work at cross-purposes. To meet her deadline, the novelist in our example was pounding away at the typewriter while furiously chain-smoking—without an ashtray. The ecologist, entering the scene, demanded that she pick up the cigarette butts off the grass. The novelist politely told him not to disturb her. The ecologist persisted in his demand. In angry frustration, the novelist tore a sheet of paper from the typewriter and threw it on the ground. The ecologist ordered her to pick up the paper.

Sometimes, however, characters accommodate each other in effecting a mutual goal; at other times, the characters are so diametrically opposed that complete avoidance is the only solution.

After a while, the novelist, whether out of frustration or caginess (a ploy to get rid of him), helped the ecologist pick up paper scraps on the beach. During analysis of the scene, we found that the novelist considered the ecologist an interesting "kooky" character for her next book. In the meantime, however, she had to work at her goal—to meet the deadline. Because the ecology freak was playing his goal so well, he gave the novelist no respite. The novelist for a moment considered drowning the ecologist but decided instead to pack up the typewriter and head for her office-beach house to finish the job—a logical and psychologically rewarding resolution.

ROLE OF THE LEADER
The primary role of the leader is to help provide a structure through which the participants themselves release their creative energies and imaginations to solve the particular improvisational problem. In helping the actors realize the char-

acters' goals, coaching should be minimal, generally restricted to helping the players concentrate on *who, what,* and *where.* The leader can also provide some technical help during the improv, perhaps by reminding the participants to "open up" to the audience, not to block each other out, to speak up, and so forth. The leader reminds the players to confront rather than merely converse. Depending on how the improvisation is going, the leader may give more or less time, introduce a built-in time clock to enhance the dramatic immediacy of a scene and ensure the clash of opposing wills, and point up an inevitable crisis. It is the role of the leader to sense how much time is needed for exploration and when and where to indicate directions that may prove fruitful. The leader can also be helpful before and after the actual improvisations.

Before the improv begins, the leader—on the spot— should edit the *where,* so that only *two* people are interacting in it. For example, it is early morning or nighttime at the beach where the novelist is working; the ecologist happens to be strolling along. Other examples: An old hotel lobby is deserted except for the two players who happen to be there (the actors must find their own motivations for being there). It is a snowy, windy day in the park, where only foolhardy or adventurous folk would venture out (our two players, of course!). Incidentally, when you prepare your own Missions Possible slips, *it is imperative that you do not include the where.* The last-minute choosing of the *where* by the class as a whole adds an extra element of challenging surprise for the two players.

After the skit has been completed, the leader moderates the discussion concerning its effectiveness. Ask questions using the ACTED ST guidelines (Chapter 6).

VARIATIONS

1. The exercise need not start off with the taped voice (although this does set up a mood of mystery and adventure). Instead of using sealed envelopes, slips of paper with the situations on them may be placed in a bag. The bag is passed around, participants reaching into it for their missions; or the bag can remain on the floor in the center of the room. Two players pick their slips and do the improv; then another two players pick their slips, and so forth.

173

2. Once an improv is in progress, the leader may spontaneously send in another actor (as a definite character) to sharpen or change the focus, heighten the drama, or clarify the conflict.

3. After one run-through, the improv can be played in different styles: as a Greek tragedy, a situation comedy, and so forth. The important thing is to capture the essence of the style without losing the basic conflict. For example, doing it as a TV soap opera, the novelist would give reams of slow, tortuous plot exposition as to why she is at the beach. As a Greek tragedy, Alice and Burt would intone in majestic dialogue with appropriately heightened gestures. As a musical comedy, the actors would sing and sway their way through the action. A TV game show would be rush, rush, rush. An improv can be carried through with one style, or there can be rapid intercutting of a variety of styles within one skit.

4. The skits can also be played in a variety of tempos—normal speed, extra fast, slow motion. To convey the feeling underneath the words, some skits can be played in gibberish or Martian-talk.

5. The class need not always be informed beforehand of the two players' *who* and *what*. In this case, the leader alone selects the *where*, and the class tries to guess the identity of the characters through the improvised action.

6. Players can take turns being leaders of the exercise. This gives them valuable experience in editing the slips of paper, coaching, and leading the evaluation.

7. Players should have opportunities to compose their own Missions Possible situations. Remember to keep the characters vital and interesting and to make their goals compelling. Keep the situations short. Repeat: Do *not* write a *where* into the situation.

8. Favorite situations can be acted by different combinations of people. Some can be tape-recorded and transcribed, to be used as the basis of an original play or assembly program.

USES

During the rehearsal of a scripted play, cast members can make up situations about their own or other characters. These

Missions Possible can be used during rehearsal, as here in a scene from *The Country Girl* by Clifford Odets performed by Long Branch High School students and directed by Vincent Borelli.

(Photo by Tom Fridy)

situations can actually occur in the play or refer to offstage action or even hypothetical situations. To illustrate, three slips might have these diverse *who*s and *what*s: You are Willy Loman (*Death of a Salesman*) and you must convince Howard to give you a job. You are a young Willy Loman, and you want Linda to marry you. You are Willy Loman, and you want your friend Charlie to move in with you. Playing Missions Possible with already created characters can help you to investigate the role further and extend your intuitive powers. In studying dramatic literature, it is conceivable that a whole host of cnaracters from different periods and representing different styles can interact with each other: King Lear confronting Hedda

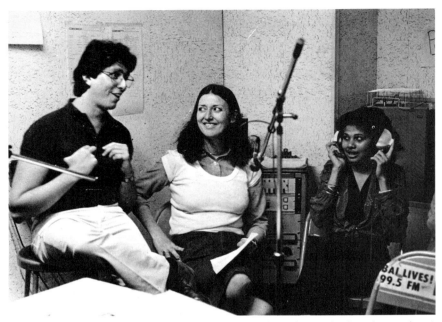

Missions Possible on the radio. Callers suggest the *who, what,* and *where* for on-the-air improvs.
(*Photo by Glen Faber*)

Gabler in Grand Central Station; Amanda Wingfield meeting Oedipus Rex in the deserted lobby of the Statler-Hilton.

Likewise, classroom subjects such as history, social studies, and current affairs can come alive and become personally meaningful to students who have the opportunity to devise and enact Missions Possible situations. In history, for example, Missions Possible can be created within a single period or may span many eras or even epochs, so that a primitive person discovering a wheel may wind up in the company of Louis Pasteur. Harriet Tubman, daring Underground Railroad agent, may find herself facing Nero, each with their own goals but playing off each other as the improvisation develops.

Wherever you use the Missions Possible exercise and its variations, you will discover that it is an enjoyable way to learn about drama. The exercise's balanced combination of planned and spontaneous activity offers a dynamic way to develop self-confidence, stretch the imagination, and cultivate intuition. As its motto, the voice on the tape you heard at the beginning of the exercise might have added: "Always expect the unexpected, but never be unprepared!"

PLAYER'S DIARY

1. Who is your favorite character in a play you have seen or read?

2. What is this character's major goal? Opposing character? Major obstacle? What is the outcome of the conflict with the opposing character?

3. What was your favorite improvisation in this chapter? Why?

4. What was your least favorite improvisation? Why?

5. Have you tried doing Twists and Turns with your friends and family at home? If so, how did it work out?

6. While playing Twists and Turns, what have you learned about your own creative potential?

7. Do you think you could evolve a play from a Twists and Turns situation?

8. What is your favorite improvisation that can be used for scripted characters?

9. What is the essential element of drama?

10. Discuss this statement: The essence of improvisation is to work together to resolve situations with conflict.

Add your own questions, thoughts, and observations.

*'Tis not the mere stage of life
but the part we play thereon
that gives the value.*

Schiller

ROLE-PLAYING 10

During our lifetimes we all play a diversity of roles: children, parents, students, teachers, workers, and members of a community. Some of these roles are acquired at birth; some we attain through long years of struggle; still others are imposed upon us by society. Some of the roles we play are beneficial in our search for identity and integrity; some serve as weapons of survival and adjustment; and some are self-denying. In order to cope with the pressures and expectations of society, many times—like the clown who is crying inside—we wear protective masks that hide our true feelings.

WHY ROLE-PLAY?

In the theater or classroom, role-playing a variety of characters helps us to explore unfamiliar life-styles and alternative ways of behavior. When we take off our own masks to wear another, we are exercising a legitimate form of self-deception under playful circumstances.

In the process of getting out of our own skins to portray others, play is perhaps our most natural method of self-expression. Our earliest means of exploring and discovering the world around us, play very often reflects our true feelings. It is no secret that young children repeat in play everything that makes a strong impression upon them in real life. In trying out diverse patterns of behavior, play is a safe way of approximating reality and testing ideas in action. In role-playing, we become what we play, and we play what we become.

Through improvisation—which by its very nature is spontaneous, immediate, and often involves the expression of gut feelings—we can obtain a heightened awareness of ourselves in relation to others. For example, two youngsters are arguing about possession of a toy. Instead of verbalizing or moralizing the conflict, the parent might ask each child on the spot to take the place of the other and give reasons as to who should claim ownership. This process is known as role reversal. Another example of role reversal involves a student who has stolen something from a classmate. Instead of merely lecturing the student about dishonesty, the imaginative teacher can devise a role-playing situation in which someone is caught stealing a radio in school. The class as a whole would then discuss what they would do about it. Hopefully, the thief would play the victim and experience, as well as articulate, what it *feels* like to be on the *receiving* end of an inappropriate act.

In practical terms, role-playing and role reversal are techniques of helping people to perceive a problem emotionally from the other person's vantage point. Participants find themselves in a situation where they must first see and then defend a position or attitude opposite to or at least different from their own. Thus, in a rehabilitation setting, wardens will role-play convicts and vice versa; in human relations, blacks and whites will role-play each other; in education, teachers and students will exchange roles, all to the end of becoming more sensitive to each other's needs and desires.

CHOOSING YOUR ROLES
AND THEMES

The source of role-playing material is abundant and right before you. The greatest resources are original ideas that spring from the imaginations of the players themselves.

You may wish to play *familiar* roles in a secure environment with the mutual support of your friends. Players may wish to explore feelings about friends and common family concerns. For example, a role reversal improvisation in which a father plays a teenage son might not only rekindle feelings of past years as a form of rear-mirror reflection but also help the player experience the creative joy of living in the here and now.

Some players may prefer to enact, for the fun of it, *unfamiliar* roles they never had a chance to play in real life—butcher, baker, banker—the list is endless. One older woman in our workshops who played a "hooker" trying to lure a customer

Role-playing is a dynamic avenue to new viewpoints. (Living Stage Company, Arena Stage, directed by Robert Alexander. Living Stage is funded by the National Endowment on the Arts.)

(Photo by Fletcher Drake)

exclaimed proudly after the improvisation, "In all my life I never dreamed I could do that!"

Finally, you may wish to project roles for the *future*, a way of "trying on life" in preparation for a new job, a change in environment, meeting new friends, dealing with changing social mores and expectations. Through playing out a situation or scene, players can simulate future possibilities.

JUST FOR STARTERS

FANTASY PROJECTIONS

You and your partners land on a new and strange planet. You desperately need something to eat in order to survive! The food (other players!) you want turns out to be alive! Communicate with this strange plant life. What do you do??? Make up other projection fantasies dealing with issues of survival.

WISHING WELL

1. Make a three-sided space with chairs. This is your wishing well.

2. One person ventures inside. In this magical space, you can be anyone or thing you wish and do anything you wish (except physical violence). Whatever you decide to do, you should do with your whole being; use the entire space. You can dance; you can fly, hide, skip; you can be *anybody* you wish.

3. Another player goes inside and does his or her thing. Do you know who he or she is? Do you care? How do you react to each other? Take the time to notice what the other person does. Does he or she intrude on your space or help? How does this affect your "inner space," how you feel? Talk *briefly* about the experience after everyone has had a chance to participate.

SAY TWO, SEE THREE

1. Each player states two roles he or she has played in life— for example, mother, son, lifeguard, community member.

2. Then the same player acts in pantomime three roles he or she would like to play—for example, tap dancer, writer, lawyer, father, and so on.

3. Discuss *briefly* what backgrounds and fantasies you have in common.

SHORT SCENES

1. Build a scene not more than five minutes long with a beginning, middle, and end, using the following situational starters:

CONFLICTING ROLES	SITUATIONAL STARTERS
referee–ball player	"You're out!"/"I'm not!"
teacher–student	"Pay attention."/"You're picking on me!"
girlfriend–boyfriend	"You can pay the check."/"Me?"
rider–cabdriver	"Pull over!"/"Nothing doing!"
grandmother–grandson	"Happy birthday!"/"This is all I get?"
tenant–landlord	"We're freezing!"/"Pay the rent!"
boss–worker	"Late again?"/"On this salary?"
wife–husband	"Who's cooking tonight?"/"Who's cooking tonight?"

Add your own:

_____	_____
_____	_____
_____	_____

2. After role reversal and discussion, replay the scenes with new players. This time add a third character for each scene. For example:

referee–ball player	"You're out!"/"I'm not!"
spectator	"Throw the bum out!"

How does the addition of each new character influence the scene and the playing of roles?

SOCIAL THEMES

The following theme-oriented hypotheticals may have as many characters as needed to make the scene "go." Scenes may last from five seconds to five minutes. The class can be divided into subgroups of three or four players each; each subgroup works on its own variation of the social theme, and the skits are informally presented for the workshop.

A social role is the patterned form of behavior, usually culturally determined, that one performs in a group. Role-playing generally implies a reciprocal relationship: student–teacher; parent–offspring; boyfriend–girlfriend, and so forth. Role-playing is theme oriented and situational: family and home themes, dating, preparing for a job interview, adjusting to a new job.

1. In role-playing, the players are given a conflict situation and are asked to play the role the situation calls for.

2. After the enactment is over, the situation is discussed. Discussion should concentrate on the sharing of feelings flowing from the improvisation: Have you ever been involved in similar situations in real life? How did you handle or react to the situation? The group is encouraged to make connections and to gain insights around family and community relationships. Through discussion, the group may clarify and test the validity of social skills, habit, and values in action. Through sharing reactions, a group member can become more aware of his or her own feelings and the effect of these feelings on others. The discussion should emphasize the validity of expressing all feelings.

3. After the discussion, the players reverse roles, repeat the situation, and gain insight into the other players' feelings. Understanding is enhanced when the players get a chance to experience both sides of the behavioral coin. In one scene, for example, a teenager who has just received his driver's license nicks his father's new car. The son and father have it out, and then the father plays the role of the teenager and vice versa.

4. Conduct a discussion of how switching roles added to each other's emotional awareness. Could the group identify with the problem and resolution or lack of a resolution?

DATING TROUBLES

One of your parents discovers that you are dating someone of another race or religion. The emotions underlying prejudice and misunderstanding—anger, frustration, guilt, resentment—may lie suppressed, submerged; or all hell may break loose. You will not know until you enact the scene. Create as many characters with specific traits as needed to explore the problem. Reverse roles; repeat scene.

Role-playing about dating problems.
(*Photo by Tom Fridy*)

ROVING REPORTER

You are a hotshot reporter from _____ Mag, exposing corruption wherever it exists. Visit different parts of your community—the school board, city hall, the country club, the jail house—and interview the key people involved in some undercover setup. Dig for the latest "dramatic dirt," whether it is a confrontation with cops or a protest parade against air pollution held at a nearby factory. Remember to reverse roles. It is important, for example, to see and feel the difficulties of being part of the police force or a member of the business community.

SUBWAY SCENE

The fare is rising, and so is your temper. You decide to do something about it, but what and with whom? Figure out a

Roving Reporter, in guise of a gossip columnist, tries to uncover Hollywood actor's problem.
(*Photo by Tom Fridy*)

specific solution to the issue of inflation as it affects you, and show it in action. In place of the subway, you can substitute

    supermarket

    gas station

    laundromat

Add your own:

_____

_____

_____

Remember to show opposing characters in conflict.

TALKING BOOKS

Improvise a dialogue between an author and the characters in his or her book. The book or story chosen should revolve around a social theme—for example, racial prejudice in *Invisible Man* by Ralph Ellison. After the enactment, remember to reverse roles. Some of the characters in the book may wish to talk with the players about what is happening in their lives.

WORLD OF WORK

You are an employer who, because of a budget crisis, has to fire three people by noon today. Who will it be and why? Call each of them in, and tell them the bad news. As a job loser, how do you feel about losing the job? What do you tell your boss, your spouse, your best friend? What changes in your gestures and facial expression did the group notice when the bad news was received?

DISTANCING TECHNIQUES

In acting out social themes, some players may be shy about revealing their feelings about an issue especially when starting. The following distancing techniques help the reluctant player become somewhat removed from the situation—better, ironically, to jump into it. As one player recalled: "I felt . . . less inhibited. . . . I was able to more readily try out new roles and life-styles, clarify old roles . . . the support from the group was great. . . ."

ANIMALS

At any point in the role-playing improvisation, become the essence of an animal or bird that captures the character you are playing. For example, during Roving Reporter, you might become a nosy newspaper owl: "Who? Who? Who? What? What?" The person playing opposite you can also assume the characteristics of the animal. Move around, and talk like the animal. Return to being a human at any time.

FUTURISM

Set the entire scene in the future, or switch to future vision at any time during the improvisation. Say you are enacting a theme from World of Work. As a parent, you want your son or daughter to get a job for the summer. Employer, you need desperately to hire someone. Son or daughter, you hate the job and want out, even before you begin the job. The players can make a mind picture of being on the moon, set a visual place, and talk gibberish (see Chapter 5), expressing feelings nonverbally. Employer, can you sense a lack of interest from the interviewee's body language? Substitute any time modality you wish, switching between past, present, and future. Tackle any current issue by setting it in another historical period—factual or fictional.

LITERARY/FILM ADAPTATIONS

Select key scenes from a film or book that focuses the idea behind the theme. For example, for Roving Reporter investigating city corruption, become characters from *All the President's Men*. Frame the idea in a few sentences, including who the characters are, where they are, and what they want from each other. For example, track down the kickbacks game in the city hospital system from an informant in a subway station.

SOLILOQUY

During any part of a scene, a player may speak a monologue aloud directly to himself or herself or to the "audience," spontaneously expressing feelings either as the character being played or as a real individual. A scene thus switches back and forth between a soliloquy and a dialogue between two characters. For example, two days before the big dance you find yourself dateless. Focus on this fact, and let your feelings flow. In direct address during any part of the improvisation, tell how you feel, using the first person: "I feel scared. Everyone's gonna think I'm an oddball, can't get a date—it makes me feel lousy. Well, what do they want? It's my first date—Mom wants me to act like a lady. Lady? I can't even get a date—I feel like a [name an animal]." You hear the phone ringing. Soliloquize for ten seconds, and pick up the phone. A leader can instruct a player to use soliloquy to gain clarification about feelings that are repressed and that help a player make a decision in a role. For example, in World of Work you are being interviewed for a job, but you are not quite sure you

In role, a player soliloquizes her feelings.
(*Photo by Leonard Lewis*)

can handle it. Making a soliloquy might help in convincing the employer of your true ability, which is buried in fear. Deal with the fear first by getting it out in the open.

ROLE-PLAYING WITH THE WHOLE GROUP

When the role-playing situation or problem is societal in nature, it is referred to as *sociodrama*. Sociodrama deals with collective problems that may be encountered in a group or community setting. In group situations with a high degree of interaction, play can help people develop trust as they work, share, and create together. Sociodrama is especially useful for training in human relations. In recent experiments, a group of factory employers wore simulated "cracked glasses" to experience the feelings of disorientation workers have on the first days of a new job. To prepare students for new roles, positions, and projected confrontations in life, a variety of sociodrama situations can be devised—meeting a prospective "in-law," for example, or facing a job interview.

Psychodrama, another dynamic form of role-playing, deals primarily with *personal* and emotional problems such as severe loss of identity, mental blocks, strong inhibitions, deep-seated frustrations, fears, and failings.

> A word of caution: *Psychodramatic enactments should be avoided unless performed by qualified practitioners under the supervision of a highly trained and experienced psychologist or psychiatrist.* To repeat: *Those areas of life that involve psychological matters of deep privacy and individual security should be avoided under* any *circumstances by unqualified practitioners.*

The topics chosen for sociodrama should in some way be related to the daily lives of the students participating. Examples include religious and racial prejudices; problems of dating in light of the changing perceptions of sex roles; peer-group problems dealing with loyalty, friendship, and cliques; parent–youth relationships, where relatively private problems can be discussed and dramatized because the roles are not related to only one individual but are attributable to a stereotyped societal role; controversial social issues such as censorship, academic freedom, dress codes, legalization of marijuana, and changing abortion laws, protest, freedom, and liberation movements; and labor–management relations.

For the player, perhaps the chief value of sociodrama is that by "becoming" another person, the individual can act out his or her true feelings about an issue without fear of punishment or reprimand. After all, you are *playing* a role; and although the shadow of reality is always present, in an atmosphere of trust and honest searching, you need not worry about paying the actual consequences of playing a particular role.

Here are some specific techniques for putting group role-playing situations into motion: Role-Playing C-C-C and my version of sociodrama, which involves a structure of dramatic debate. Both techniques require a warm-up session.

WARM-UP GAMES

Preferably, the games utilized before the enactment of a role-playing situation should involve the whole group and be non-verbal. The goal of a warm-up is to get the group involved and interacting. The players may select from the following for a ten- to fifteen-minute warm-up. A good way to break the ice of any possible existing tension is with some joyful spontaneous play and movement. Move around the room to the beat of a drum. When the drumbeat periodically stops, say "hello" to your immediate neighbor. At different pauses, say "hello" in gibberish or in complete silence with your arm or nose or other parts of the body. Walk around the room as a puppet or as a stiff wooden soldier, and say "hello" with eyes only. Play a game of stylized tag, where the players imitate the movements of "It," who tries to catch the rest (no running allowed!). Write your name in space. Be a candle, and melt to the ground; with other group members, twist yourselves into a giant knot, and untangle yourselves from one another. Crawl along the floor with your eyes closed, and touch one another in complete silence; be aware of skin texture, hair, and clothing.

Pass your names around while sitting in a circle; pass around a pet in pantomime. Pass around one sound, and transform it into other sounds; pass around faces, and transform them. Passing a ball around, tell a continuation fantasy story. Build an exciting world in pantomime. With the group, sing some nursery rhymes, and act them out. Perform some trust exercises. Share a brief fantasy. In a circle, take turns guiding players who have their eyes closed into the center; with the total trust and concentration of the group, lift a person into the air and rock him or her gently. Or have a player, keeping his or her body rigid, fall into the arms of fellow players in a tight circle. Play the mirror game in pairs, trios, quintets, octets. Make a machine.

ROLE-PLAYING C-C-C

CONFLICT IS THE KEY: FIRST ENACTMENT

In this exercise two or three players at a time enact a scene while the rest of the group becomes active observers. Any of the exercises in this chapter can trigger an extended role-playing situation.

Conflict is the heart of drama and the key to role-playing. Participants assume the different *characters* necessary to play out and, hopefully, resolve the conflict. For example, on one confrontation, a "wife" wants to use her savings to take a trip around the world. Her "husband," on the other hand, doesn't want to spend the money on anything but the necessities of life; thus the basis for a role-playing situation.

1. Before the scene starts, each player should close his or her eyes and review mentally *who* he or she is, *what* he or she wants in the scene (in this case, to convince each other to take the trip), and *where* they are (in the kitchen nook).

2. The scene is enacted. The scene may take anywhere from a few to five minutes or so. The scene should aim for a dramatic outcome of the basic conflict.

3. After the enactment, the players are asked how they feel, both as characters and players. A *brief* discussion takes place focusing on the conflict and its resolution or lack of resolution.

CHOICES: FURTHER ENACTMENTS

While the actors role-play these characters, different *choices* of behavior come into play. During one enactment, for example, one may not give the other a chance to talk, so intent is she or he on scoring points.

1. If these characters are not able to resolve the conflict, other pairs of players might assume the same roles to show how they would approach and resolve the conflict.

2. In another enactment, both spouses may argue a point, with neither really listening to the other. In still another version of the scene, both may learn to compromise their positions somewhat, so as to live in peace and harmony with each other. The wife may suggest half a trip around the world, or the husband may loosen up the purse strings a bit.

3. A lively discussion should take place after each enactment. *Observers are encouraged to be active listeners.* Going around the circle, each observer is asked to state what he or she saw in the scene, to discuss *details,* not merely to offer subjective views. For example: "I saw the husband turn his head when his wife brought up the trip. Then she raised her voice. Then he got up from the table. . . ."

4. After the details have been filled in, each observer is asked if he or she believed the scene was real. One observer might say, "They would try to reason more with each other rather than just shouting." So then the observer (or another volunteer) would replay the scene but this time, playing a reasonable husband to see what would happen.

CONSEQUENCES: DISCUSSION AND EXTENSIONS

After several scenes have been enacted, conduct a discussion concerning the *consequences* of the behavioral choices. For example, what will it mean if either party gives in a little? What will the outcome be if a note of compromise is struck?

How will other people in the lives of the husband and wife be affected by the outcome? A lively discussion will probably ensue, and a member of the group can moderate the proceedings and summarize the thoughts of the group.

As *extensions* of the role-playing scene, be mindful of the following variations:

1. Any of the characters might meet with a friend to discuss what has happened or what to do. Thus, the wife might meet with her sister (another player called up on the spot) to discuss how to handle the situation with her husband. The husband might meet with a friend or member of the family.

2. Any of the characters might meet with someone who could conceivably be connected with the outcome of the scene if such a meeting will contribute to communication and understanding. For example, either of the parties might meet with a travel agent to find out more about this projected trip.

3. At any time during the improvisation, a player may be asked to do a soliloquy (see "Distancing Techniques" earlier in this chapter) to express the inner feelings and gut reactions of the character.

Add your own:

_____

_____

_____

SOCIODRAMATIC DEBATE

This technique differs from Role-Playing C-C-C in two major respects. The class as a whole selects the role-playing situation, and the class as a whole acts out the situation.

1. *After the warm-up, the sociodrama situation is selected.* Suggestions from players are listed on the board and are voted on until, by a process of elimination, only *one* suggestion remains. The leader should make clear that if any of the topics to be debated are personally unacceptable to any of the players, that player may simply eliminate the topic. For example, in one graduate workshop, one of the topics was: "Should a marriage contract be initiated instead of a marriage license?" One student had recently gone through a bitter divorce and had no stomach to debate the issue at that time. The topics should be posed as questions—for example: Should marijuana be legalized? Should college tuition be eliminated? Should grades be required? Should students have the right to wear what they want? Should men and women have equal rights?

2. *The role-playing situation is set up.* Say the last question—"Should men and women have equal rights?"—is selected for enactment. First of all, the leader and players revise the question so that it is realistically presented and has the greatest relevancy and dramatic potential for the participants. The group decides that the question should be rephrased: "Should men and women be *required by law* to have equal rights as well as responsibilities?"

The leader now asks all those in the class who believe that men and women *should* be required by law to have equal rights and responsibilities to sit together on one side of the room. Those who believe that men and women should *not* be required by law to have equal rights and responsibilities are asked to sit on the other side of the room. The leader then announces that all those who took the position that men and women should have equal rights and responsibilities will support the position *against* equal rights and responsibilities for men and women. Those who stated that they were against the position will argue *for* equality during the role-playing situation. Now we literally have two rows of opponents facing each other ready for debate.

Social prototypes are assigned next. On *each* side of the position, players volunteer for the following roles: a member of the clergy, a lawyer, a medical authority, a social worker, women's liberation representative/men's group representative, mothers, fathers, offspring, college students, legislators, and any other social/occupational roles deemed necessary. The leader also asks one player to serve as moderator.

The leader, with the help of the group, structures the debate so that it will be a *dramatic* encounter. In this case, the leader mentions that a women's group has called for new legal action and that a special blue-ribbon panel of distinguished citizens from the community have been called together to air the problem. The moderator, as special advisor to the governor, will chair the meeting (the leader can serve as an aide to the moderator). It is always a good idea to build a "dramatic clock" into improvisational role-playing to ensure that the presentation is dynamic and has a sense of urgency. In this case, the moderator mentions that the governor intends to convene the state legislators in one hour and therefore *must* have this panel's recommendations at the end of the hour.

Before starting the sociodramatic debate, the leader asks everyone to review mentally (and *in character!*) the stated public position he or she will be espousing. The leader reminds the players that they will have more fun with their newly created roles if they are completely serious about enacting them. All players should attempt to get out of their own skin and get *into* the minds, actions, and feelings of their characters—even if the position the characters take is not the one the students themselves would ordinarily uphold. Remember, the purpose of role-playing is to see and defend a position normally different than one's own personal feelings. As in

An intense moment during a sociodramatic debate.
(*Photo by Mary Alfieri*)

Bag-O'-Drama (Chapter 11) it will help you to concentrate on the goals of the character and think of one or two physical or vocal characteristics that will help give the role texture—for example, a Southern congressman, an aging psychiatrist, an outspoken social worker, and so forth.

3. *The role-playing situation is enacted.* The moderator pounds the gavel and summarizes why the panel has been assembled; the presentation is on the way! The moderator (perhaps with some help from the leader-as-aide) keeps the debate flowing, making sure all sides are alternately heard from. It is a good idea for the moderator to ask the participants to stand up, give their name, and identify their position before speaking, such as Dr. F. Green from the Equal Rights Counseling Service, or Mrs. Mabel Jones, a newlywed who feels her duty is in the home, and the like. All speeches should be short, keeping to the point. The moderator makes sure there are no emotional outbursts, although these can be part of the drama and fun of the enactment. So, too, are unexpected diversions such as protestors appearing from the hearing room's peanut gallery opposing "compulsory" laws or stand-up confrontations between opposing panelists.

4. *Discussion takes place after the enactment.* Discussion questions include: Were the participants satisfied with the decision reached by the moderator? Were the characters believable and convincing in their roles? Why? Why not? How did the participants feel about their parts and stated positions? What alternative courses of behavior were suggested by the dramatized interaction? (For example, was the issue clouded over or sharpened by the element of compulsion? Should the phrasing of the question have been limited to equality between husbands and wives rather than between all men and women? Why? Why not?) Keep the discussion honest and constructive.

5. *The role-playing situation is reenacted with role reversal.* With the exception of the moderator, all players switch their positions. Literally and physically, all those who were in favor of equal rights and responsibilities for men and women now sit in the chairs of those who were opposed to them; those who were opposed cross the room to sit in the chairs of those

Video feedback aids discussion after a sociodramatic debate.

(*Photo by Claudia M. Caruana*)

who were in favor. The social roles for each player remain the same. This time, however, Dr. F. Green, formerly of the Equal Rights Counseling Service, will be staunchly opposed to a position of equality and will think of reasons to support the position; Mrs. Mabel Jones, the newlywed, now wants to work outside instead of staying cooped up in a house all day. The dramatic situation (the report to the governor) virtually remains the same, incorporating any qualitative changes that may have cropped up in the previous playing.

6. *More discussion takes place.* How did you feel arguing both sides of the issue? What did you learn? Did playing one position help you to prepare for later defending the opposite point of view? Did you acquire any new insights and understanding about the problem? Did cultural aspects come into play? Were you able to get into the feelings and emotions underneath the statistics of the issue? What additional research must be done to understand better the dynamics of the social problem?

These are the six steps in my version of sociodrama. Of course, there is always room for further experimentation. Role-playing has existed as long as people have, and new variations are always welcome. Much joy in playing your many parts!

POSSIBLE TOPICS TO BE DEBATED IN ROLE-PLAYING

1. Should a marriage contract be renewed every five years?
2. Should certain "hard" drugs be decriminalized?
3. Should there be a popular vote exclusively to elect a president?
4. Should prostitution be legalized?
5. Should euthanasia be legalized?
6. Should abortion laws be changed?

Add your own topics:

_____

_____

_____

Role-playing is indeed a very popular activity. It affords the opportunity for people to deal with real problems loaded with conflict in a creative and constructive manner. It opens possibilities for enjoying the freedom to fantasize about a better and more beautiful world and to dramatize realistic approaches to those ideals. You will discover that although players initially join a group for a variety of reasons, underlying them all will be the need to communicate their own uniqueness. That is why their improvisations are often derived from their own personal life experiences. Role-playing thus gives people a real chance to express themselves openly, to reveal a sense of their own uniqueness with dignity and pride.

PLAYER'S DIARY

1. What was your *favorite* role? Why?

2. What was your least favorite role? Why?

3. What roles of the others in your group did you most enjoy? Why?

4. Is it possible to have role-playing situations without conflict? Why do you say this?

5. Do you remember the conflict in your favorite role-playing enactment? How was the conflict developed? How was it resolved?

6. Did you learn anything about your feelings while participating in role-playing? Can you state what you learned?

7. How did you feel about the social issue you debated in sociodramatic debate before you began?

8. How did you feel about the issue after reversing your role?

9. Was it easy or hard to reverse your role? Why?

10. What role-playing activities do you think children would enjoy doing?

Add your own questions, thoughts, and observations.

Chance favors the prepared mind
Louis Pasteur

Play out the play.
Shakespeare, *Henry IV*

PLAY-MAKING 11

A large and exciting part of improvisational activity is the discovery of the process of conflict and confrontation between characters. The irony and challenge of play-making is that players—to discover and imaginatively resolve confrontation—work together, create together, and through this process learn from one another. After all, they have created the material from the wellspring of their existence and dramatic imaginations, so it follows that the sharing and caring will be very deep.

UNDERSTANDING GOALS: PROCESS AND PRODUCT

When an improvisational play is primarily for the players' growth—expressing themselves to satisfy their own creative needs—it is considered *process centered*. In this case, there is

201

no audience except for the other players in the class or group.

If, on the other hand, the purpose of the improvisational play is to present the created material for the entertainment of an audience, the activity is considered *product centered*. Product work here is the end result of the process, the "done" of the "doing." Whereas process work is ongoing and continually evolving, product work declares that a finished result has been reached. But even with a "finished result," continued creative revisions are inevitable. In product-centered activity, costumes, makeup, lighting, and scenery may be used in the presentations that are rehearsed and polished.

If an improvisation is designed for the stage, sometimes the most enjoyable aspect is the rehearsal of the process—the actual creating—which will long remain in the memories of the performers. Whether an improvisation is process centered or product centered, structures always exist to help shape the free-flowing creative impulses that evolve from the imaginations and investigations of the players.

FROM SIMPLE TO COMPLEX: AN ILLUSTRATION

Consider the simple exercise found at the beginning of this book, of rhyming a word and then pantomiming it. Did you rhyme the word *go* with *row* and imagine you were in a boat sailing to far-off Cathay? Or did you rhyme it with *flow* and imagine you were a river winding its way through Africa?

If you were going to take this improvisation further, you could derive a play from it. For example, let us say you rhymed the word with *show* and then mentally added the word *off.* Let's say you are a famous weight lifter (*who*), and your goal (*what*) is to lift the heaviest weights in the world. *Why?* Perhaps you are a show-off in a contest, or perhaps you have accepted a challenge for money that you can do it. *When* and *where* does the skit take place? On Coney Island, just before closing time, to establish a sense of immediacy and urgency. *With whom?* Here is where relationships can turn into conflict, the essence of drama.

The On-the-Spot Players planning a skit.
(*Photo by Leonard Lewis*)

When performers do an improvisation for the stage, sometimes the most enjoyable part is the rehearsal—the actual creating.
(*Photo by Leonard Lewis*)

Say your pantomime partner rhymed *go* with the word *woe. Who* is he or she? Let's say a circus owner. His or her goal (*what*) is to fire some of the performers. *Why?* Business is so bad! *When* and *where?* Same place and time—the midway just before closing. This place is agreed upon by the two players. *Who* gets in the way? Both do, actually, as you both actively pursue your goals. As the weight lifter, you might want more time to prove you can set a new record, thus ensuring that you will hold onto your job and feed your family. The owner, on the other hand, has to fire you to save money and thus feed *his* or *her* family. How will this conflict be resolved? Will there be additional complications? This could be worked out conceptually beforehand or be developed further through improvisations. Perhaps new characters will be needed to round out the theme of human values versus monetary values. It is possible that a whole play could develop from a simple word that was rhymed.

DISCOVERING STIMULI

The stimuli that set off creative plays can be words as in the example just given; or sights, sounds, colors, pictures, stories, and poems, examples of which have already been given throughout this text.

As one player, John de Clef Piniero, noted, ideas are usually selected in the context of "definite choices among indefinite possibilities." It is not really a question of finding an idea but of choosing the right one from so many available. Ideas, in fact, are all around you in

- *Shapes—animate and inanimate*
- *Spaces—interior and exterior*
- *Situations—personal and impersonal, real and imaginary*

Here is a step-by-step example of how to devise a play based on props.

BAG-O'-DRAMA

1. *After the brief warm-up period, the participants are divided into groups of five or six players each.* It is best to mix the players by having them count off, the 1s forming one group, the 2s forming another group, and so forth. This random distribution is not as impersonal as it may sound. Randomization prevents unnecessary bickering about who will play with whom and puts the emphasis on the creating itself.

2. *A bag containing simple props* (about a half-dozen will do) *is distributed to each group, which consists of about a half-dozen players.* The contents of a typical bag, for example, might include a pipe, a book, beads, a hat or scarf, a bar of soap, a paper plate. Each bag contains different props.

3. *While the contents of the bags are still unknown to the players, follow these simple instructions:*

- Using as many of the props as you wish (you can even use the bag), your group will make up a short skit or play about five minutes long. The props can be used as they are or can be made to represent something else; for example, a dictionary can be that or a Bible; the bar of soap can be a cannister of tear gas; the scarf can be that or a diaper or whatever you wish. Additional props in the play can be mimed.

- You will have about ten minutes to make up the play. Work together and share ideas. The skit can be based on a real-life, fictitious, or even fantasy situation, as long as it touches on a problem of interest to the players. Beware of selecting a real-life situation that is so emotionally charged or has taken place so recently that it clouds the objective distance and detachment needed to enact it.

- At this point, the leader may suggest, as an *option*, that all the skits have a common setting (such as a living room) or a common theme (dating, for example) or a parallel time modality. (For example, if each group is enacting a skit about women's liberation, one group could do me in the

Former Paperbag Player Betty Osgood creating a character from newspapers and boxes.

(*Photos by Harout Merigan*)

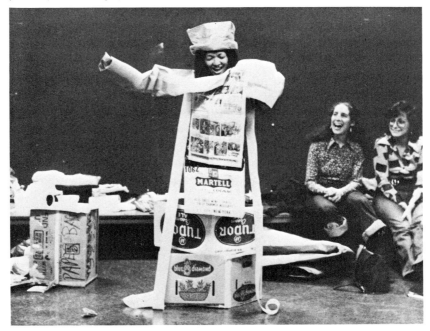

present; another group could present a scene from the past; and another could project a situation into the future.) These options may not be at all necessary, and often it is best to allow the creative juices to flow unimpeded in terms of skit content.

- Make sure the skits have a simple but *strong* conflict. Preferably, the skit should have a beginning, middle, and end. Plan especially how you will *end* your play. Discuss what the central character's main goal and problem is and what obstacles and characters block achievement of the goal.

4. *The bags are opened. The players create the skits.* The leader can count down the planning time (three minutes to go, two minutes, thirty seconds, and so on) to enhance the psychological tension needed for creativity. Do *not* take more than ten or twelve minutes to make up the skit, or you will start constructing a three-act play. If you have a basic structure, spontaneous ideas will develop during the course of playing. Structurally, during the planning stage, you should think about *who* you are, *where* the action takes place (it is best to confine the action to one setting), and *what* your main goals are. It is also helpful for each player to think of one physical and verbal character trait that will illustrate and define the character.

5. *Before the presentation of each skit, players comprising the "audience" are encouraged to be good observers and listeners.* The focus during observation should be on isolating the dramatic problem in the skit and on discussing how the problem was or was not resolved.

6. *During the actual playing of each skit, the leader continues to coach from the sidelines, making sure he or she does not impede the players' spontaneous creativity.* This coaching should be limited to technical considerations (talk up, concentrate on your goals, play the *where*, don't block each other out, two minutes left, and so forth). The leader should always keep in mind that the emphasis in the beginning is on the process and not on a polished performance.

7. *Discussion takes place after each skit is enacted.* The dis-

Bag-O'-Drama—planning . . .

and playing.
(*Photos by Leonard Lewis*)

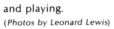

cussion should be honest and constructive; each player's contribution should be valued; and differences in approach
should be noted and accepted. The players should try to pin-
point the dramatic conflict the characters presented; how did
the characters solve the particular problem? How did it feel to
be a particular character? Could others *identify* with the character and his or her problems? What alternative ways of behavior might the characters have chosen to resolve the
problem? Did the players work together? Show imagination
and concentration? Players should take turns leading the brief
evaluation after each play.

Add your own questions for evaluation:

_____

_____

_____

All sorts of props provoke the imagination.
(*Photo courtesy of Milton Polsky*)

A Word about the Props: The key to why Bag-O'-Drama works so well is found in the security the props give the players during the planning and role-playing of the skits. First of all, the props trigger suggestions for the characters, situations, and places. It is always instructive and fun to ask how the groups got their ideas *after* the skits have been enacted. For example, for one group, a small box of Rice Krispies set into motion a serious play set at the family breakfast table about a girl who refuses to go to school that day. A scarf and hippie beads triggered a funny skit about a grandmother who befriends her radical grandson about to be expelled from college. A button and newspaper suggested a Bag-O'-Drama about setting up an underground newspaper in high school.

Secondly, any nervous tension about "performing" is somehow magically displaced onto the props themselves. In a way, the props almost become another character, saying: "Use me any way you want—I am here for your imagination to take over." And your imagination will go to work as the props become other objects or are worn as costumes. Finally, the props give the actor something concrete to do, and acting—among other things—is doing.

Some props yield ideas for familiar roles.
(*Photo by Jonathan Ishie*)

A PLAY BASED ON A
STORY OR SONG

Another possibility is to modernize an old story or song and give it a headline. One group used the Old English ballad, "Lord Randall," which is about the mysterious death of a young knight who was in love with a maiden.

> Oh, I fear you are poisoned, Lord Randall, my son . . .
> Oh, yes, I'm poisoned, mother; make my bed soon,
> For I'm sick at the heart, and I fain would lie down.

Various facts about knighthood were discussed by the group. It was learned, for example, that the chief chivalric virtues were piety, honor, valor, and loyalty to one's mistress. A knight's love life was largely platonic. As a rule, only a virgin or another man's wife could be the chosen object (and subject) of chivalrous love. The group also discussed aspects of medie-

"O, I fear you are poisoned, Lord Randall, my son. . . ."
(*Photo by W. M. Edwards*)

val times that could have affected the narrative song, but the thing that really set the collective mind in motion was this headline:

LORD RANDALL FEARED DEAD!

The class broke up into groups and presented plays attempting to answer the question of how Lord Randall *really* died. The "drama detectives" responses included Lord Randall being poisoned by his lady's jealous lord; by his other sweetheart, who poisoned Lord Randall and herself; by his own hand; and even by his mother, who feared that Lord Randall had an incurable case of the plague. These possibilities, not in the original song, all became part of the invented subtext. The class learned a great deal about English literature, history, and customs as well as play-making. Contribute your own suggestions for play-making based on a favorite story, ballad, pop song, or newspaper headline.

Add your own story suggestions:

_____

_____

_____

ADDITIONAL PREMISES FOR PLAY-MAKING

Any number of premises deriving from improvisations you have already done can serve as a basis for a play. For example, the image of a magical guitar *evolving from* a Twist and Turn exercise (Chapter 8) was the premise for a collective creation (with script devised through improvisations) performed by one group of players. The plot of the musical, *A Ticket or a*

Tune, concerned a young man and woman in the park who lose a pawnshop ticket that would enable them to reclaim the magical guitar. The ensemble first created a playground jungle gym with their bodies and with sounds. Half of the ensemble then changed into the characters visiting the park; seconds later, all transformed into a music store, becoming the fixtures and instruments. The mysterious proprietress of the music store sends the two friends on a journey to find either the ticket or the tune the guitar plays. If they cannot find the tune by the end of the day, all the musical instruments (really people who have been enchanted by the store's owner) will rust from lack of use. This is the "stake" of the show, enabling the audience to root for the two friends to succeed. In the course of the odyssey, the cast is transformed into many environments and characters, including a magical subway train, an underwater kingdom of human sea creatures, sky divers, and other improvised characters. No set was required because the actors created the objects, environments, and atmospheres of the play. The cast did wear simple white T-shirts with musical notes on them.

Perhaps you have a recurring dream or fantasy that would inspire such a story. A sensory touch exercise could stimulate a dramatization of "King Midas and the Golden Touch." The blind walk exercise could serve as a springboard for enacting Helen Keller's story. The subjects are as vast as the universe, open to whatever interests you have and whatever you wish to express.

CREATING A SCENARIO

A play is a sequence of situations in which characters show who they are, how they feel, and what they do in reaching a definite goal. When the goal of the central character is blocked by one or more opposing characters, obstacles are created that produce conflict and dramatic tension.

Plot is the way you tell your story, not only in words but also in *dramatic actions*. It is the interweaving of characters and situations that builds to a dramatic outcome. How do you reach that outcome? One working method is to begin with a central character who has a strong goal, focus the central conflict, and then resolve the conflict.

THE SCENARIO:
WHO–WHAT–WHERE CHART

The scenario is the outline of your play. It is a written summary of the story—a step-by-step conceptualization of each scene as the dramatic action of the play unfolds—describing the sequence of events, the characters and their movement, the time and the place. You may write the scenario in sentences and paragraphs or in an outline format using brief phrases.

List the following progression: *who* will be in the scene, *what* will happen, and *where* the action will take place. In three vertical columns on a sheet of paper, fill in the outline with the specifics as they emerge through conscious deliberation about the problem as well as spontaneous improvisation. Here is the start of the scenario for *A Ticket or A Tune:*

WHO	WHAT	WHERE
Jerry Bernadette	Jerry is moving away. His close friend Bernadette has a surprise for him and gives him a ticket, which will enable him to pick up the surprise. Jerry puts the ticket in a safe place, his shoe, and both head off to song shop.	Park playground
Bernadette Jerry Lynda	Jerry can't find ticket to claim guitar. Song shop	

WHO	WHAT	WHERE
Music boxes	owner demands either ticket or tune. Music boxes, in defiance of Lynda, come downstage to offer their help, but each has wrong tune. Lynda has to have either the ticket or the tune by five o'clock, or music boxes will remain machines instead of turning back into people.	
Jerry Bernadette Pair of pickpockets People on train	Jerry finds the ticket in his shoe. They hurry to go on train to take them back to shop, but while on train, Jerry's ticket is stolen by a pair of pickpockets. The train transforms into a Magic Train that takes them on the rest of adventures....	Park/Train

Some write scene-by-scene breakdowns on 3-by-5-inch cards and shift them around until a plot takes shape. Shorthand, doodles, notes to yourself are all helpful. You can construct a chart using *objective* (the major character's goal) —*obstacles* (the central conflict)—*outcome* (resolution of conflict) as your outline. Diagrams such as

central character→obstacles→goal←opposing character

can be helpful as well. You may also think of colors, objects, and music to help you structure and discover the texture of your play: varying moods of scenes, contrapuntal themes, melody through lines, and so forth.

If the play originates as a collective creation—springing from the ideas of the group—then listen to others, and understand their concepts with the same interest and perception you use to communicate your own ideas. In a collective creation, as the ideas of the group coalesce into dramatic form, there are usually one or two players (it could be the director, or the playwright, or a player who has a sharp sense of dramatic structure) who assume the role of editing the ideas into a unified dramatic whole. You may discover that one or more of the players are especially good at directing. Others may be good energizers, organizers, inspirers, moderators, or coordinators.

GUIDELINES FOR A PRODUCT-CENTERED PLAY

1. Review the theme, plot, and structure of your play.

2. Determine which events, situations, and characters are necessary to evoke a dramatic expression that is understandable, simple, and exciting. Ask yourself especially why the plot begins when it does. Why today and not yesterday or tomorrow? What is there in the action of the story to change the status so that the play begins *now?* In *Hamlet*, for example, his father's death makes him return home, and the action begins. In *Death of a Salesman*, Biff returns from the West, causing Willy to reevaluate the contradictions in his own life. In short, what action in the present precipitates the events that follow?

3. List all the characters involved in the play, and sufficiently explain who they are. Include their overall objective—what they want to achieve during the play.

4. Review the place, or if it is a multiscenic play, describe the locale of each scene.

5. Review the time of year and hour for each scene. Know what is important about that *particular* time that might help you create a more effective play (e.g., dark night, dawn, a hot afternoon).

6. Clarify the scope of each dramatic segment. Depending upon the size and depth of your creation—whether it is a five-minute improvisation or a longer play—decide what *specifically* happens in each act, scene, event, and action.

7. Review your scenario, and check the dramatic emphasis of each character and event and their relationship to one another. Make sure the play has at least one main character the audience can care about, a simple yet strong central conflict, and a progression of dramatic actions that culminate in a climax and resolution. Review the dramatic question, the play's major crisis (turning point), and climax (the play's high point).

CHECKLIST

- *Whose play* is it? (*central character*)
- Why does the plot *begin* when it does? (*What incident triggers the action and what happens to the central character?*)
- What is the *central conflict?* (*obstacles blocking central character's goal*)
- Is the *crisis* or turning point clearly established?
- What is at *stake?* (*Why do we care about the central character?*) *Visible stake:* This is a prop or place that shows the stake in action (letter of Transit in *Casablanca,* ruby slippers in *Wizard of Oz,* the bridge Tony has to cross into Manhattan in *Saturday Night Fever,* the poker game in *The Odd Couple*).
- Is the *climax* or high point of the play clearly established?
- Is the *resolution* of *conflict* clearly and believably established?

Once you determine the major goals of the characters and the scope of the action (the incidents leading to the climactic scene), you can get deeper into the story so that the bare bones of the outline will be fleshed out through revision and rehearsing. You may have to go through several revisions, constantly pruning the material in the process of discovering where the play is going. One clue triggers other creative responses. The process, to be sure, will involve some uncertainty, including false starts and trial and error. So stay with it as you think about the characters who will comprise your play, and search for the structure that will frame and focus the incidents of the plot and give depth to your characters.

VISUAL ELEMENTS

A flick of the hand, a sudden smile, the flash of an eye, and the most subtle variations of touch can transport players and audience alike to a myriad of places and times. A stage or a street, a platform or playground—all serve equally well if imaginative use is made of what is available. Primitive men and women, ancient Greeks and Romans, medieval strollers, and zany improvisational *Commedia dell'arte* players of the sixteenth century all performed outdoors, and so can modern practitioners of improvisation. Ordinary playground equipment can become the backdrops and settings for interesting improvisations. An outdoor gym, for example, can easily be transformed into a royal palace; a seesaw becomes a boat; a slide, a mountain slope.

It is not within the scope of this book to discuss sets, properties, costumes, or lighting fully, but the physical production may range from a simple, bare stage to a complete set with turntables. Sets for the play need not be elaborate, and realistic pictorial settings need not be used at all. It would be preferable to use symbolic settings that *suggest* the place and have the actors create the environment through minimal props and the use of pantomime. Remember, of course, that a few banners or tapestries or a coat of arms can transform a bare stage into a palace. A simple screen-flat painted to indicate a stained window and a few benches suggest a church setting. If you are presenting your play to others, the director and designer may try to find a symbolic and suggestive theatrical stroke that will employ the details of a larger whole; in other words, they search for a scenic metaphor. For example, in a musical mime I directed, *Hot Headlines,* designer Ernest Smith's scenic metaphor of a collage of newsprint on screens was employed to convey the flavor of a show that dealt with a magazine review of newspaper departments: Angry Letters to the Editor (gibberish), Lost and Found (fantasy mime skits), astrological signs (sono-mime), story theater skits, and so on. (See Appendix C for format.)

For variety, consider the use of different levels made from plywood platforms. They can be of the same height and different widths and lengths. Smaller platforms can be set on larger ones. A good background drape, if needed, can be made from unbleached muslin, cotton flannel, or monk's cloth stretched together and dyed soft blue. Look for secondhand materials that can be transformed imaginatively into stage materials. You can create other designs representing the play's range of emotional feelings by experimenting with different inks on slides. These slides are then projected onto a wall, screen, scrim, or on the bodies of the actors themselves.

Opera on the spot created by Jolantha Kerschnagel and Tony Clark. A scene from the opera *Die Fledermaus.*
(*Photo by Glen Faber, courtesy of the Brookdale Drama Project.*)

IMPROVISATION AND
AUDIENCE PARTICIPATION

STAGE

There are a number of kinds of audience involvement that can take place during a play. The first is the *direct* request for ideas. For example, actors in Proposition Circus, the improvisational ensemble directed by Allan Albert, ask for a favorite song and proceed to become the musicians playing the instruments in mime—first as a marching band, then as a swinging jazz band, and so forth. The company asks for three different emotions and elicits responses from the audience. Then the cast proceeds to make an Emotion Machine. The ensemble later asks the audience for something lost, something they are afraid of, and something they would like to be. With these three items in mind, the actors perform a story theater "fractured" tale with a narrator improvising the story and the rest of

CoMixCo enact skit based upon audience suggestions combining fantasy mime and verbal conflict with classical fairy tale.
(*Photo by Peter Munch*)

the company becoming the environment, characters, and objects (including the three supplied by the audience) in the story.

A most interesting form of audience participation is commonly known as the Brian Way method, which originated in England over twenty years ago with Brian Way (also the author of a fascinating text, *Development Through Drama*) but has only gained momentum in the United States since the early 1970s. In this method, the audience—children, in this case— are brought into a structured play, which has either been written by a playwright-or developed by a company of actors and director through collective improvisation. The children actually help move the story along by becoming, for example, a park into which the hero can escape or rivers and mountains to prevent the villains from capturing the hero, or by bringing mimed objects to some peasant's house so that his family will not starve.

The Park Players, directed by Milton Polsky, involve the youngsters in the action. (*Photo by Bob Cannistraci*)

The true test of audience participation is always this: Would the play work equally well without the participation? Does the audience feel the *need* to be involved in terms of the play's action and dramatic suspense? Because children often react to the action and want to be involved naturally and spontaneously with it, much of the involvement is effected through pantomime. Sounds and minimal dialogue may be used as well.

RADIO

Radio is a marvelous medium for involving an audience. The On-the-Spot Players asked for radio requests when they performed on WBAI in New York. "You give us some sounds, ideas, words, and we'll change them into something else—on the spot—we'll become characters, get conflicts, and resolve them within a dramatic form." One such radio request might call for a suggestion for a sound machine. Radio responses called in by listeners might be for a city or country machine, which the ensemble then does on the spot. Other radio requests might ask listeners to name (1) a famous name and (2) a place for the face. A radio response for the first category might be Reggie; and for the second, a ball park. Then listeners might call in (3) a time and/or season.

For example, a skit opened up in the present between Reggie and an umpire arguing over a call. Switching into the future, the umpire shouted, "You're out—says so right here on my instant replay center!" (Sounds made by group.) Another radio request: Switch to the year 3000. A new character, a robot umpire in an atomic-driven car enters the scene and bleeps that Reggie is safe—according to the "droid's teleplay right angle."

Open-ended role-playing skits involving such topics as junk food and staying out late were also very popular.

The ensemble told continuation stories (Chapter 8), enacted sound transformation and Twists and Turns, and created on-the-spot sound effects to poetry they had created earlier after playing Water-Woods-Window (Chapter 1) and Blind Walk (Chapter 2).

A favorite radio request was changing the *who–what–where* to different places and time modalities. For example, two characters are arguing over who is going to use the only available dryer in a laundromat. Cut to radio request: Medieval days—same people but now arguing over one last stone at river bank. "Pardon me, humble maiden, but this stone is mine and is already occupied by me. . . ."

The group learned that during the actual playing, "you say and do things you never dreamed you would do during the planning and rehearsal stages because the energy and concentration were not present in the same way as they are before an audience." And so, the best preparation for improvisational acting is an open, alert mind ready to act and react with the group.

When you are in a radio studio, the program director will acquaint you with what to do with mike placement and what not to do, as well—such as staying too close or far away from the mike, rustling paper, coughing, and the like. It is a good

Radio improvisations involve the audience. The players sing "What Do You Do?" in their radio version of TV format.
(*Photo by Glen Faber*)

idea to bring some signs and coordinated hand signals along to the studio: Don't overlap, speed up, slow down, wind-up, speak clearly, and cut!

TELEVISION

WHAT DO YOU DO?

This is a total participation show for television.*

Format: An ensemble of actors onstage improvise short situations or skits. These skits involve at least one member of the audience, who either comes onstage in the studio or is integrated in some other way, perhaps right from his or her seat. Each week there is a new topic based on a theme, setting (place), prop, or character. These weekly "themes" include "World of Work," "Public Places," "Relationships," "School Days," and "Fantasies." Each skit is done in an appropriate theater style: musical comedy, suspense, slapstick, horror movie, Greek tragedy, and so on. Say "World of Work" is selected as the weekly theme. The following skit is chosen:

- *Title: Same Tomb, Next Year*
- *Style:* Horror Movie
- *Situation:* You are working as Dracula's bookkeeper but dislike the night shift, so you have been looking for a new job. The new job you have found offers advancement but no salary increase. You accept. When you give notice to Count Dracula, he offers you a substantial salary increase—$4,000 more than your new job.

1. The players enact the skit to a certain open-ended point.
2. Four responses are flashed on home screen:

- Take the new job anyway.
- Stay with the Count, who needs new blood, but get more money.

* "What Do You Do?" was collectively devised by Thomas Bahring, Vincent Borelli, Thomas Clark, Richard Jude, Martha Denis, Jonathan Eisen, Jolantha Kerschnagel, Florence Reinstein, Antonia Sisti, Jennifer Vermont, Janet Youngs, and Milton Polsky (director).

WHAT DO YOU DO?

Words and Music by
JONATHAN EISEN

With energy

G / C / G

It's up to you what do you do?

C / G

It's up to you what do you do? As

Am   Bm   C   D7   Am   Bm

doc - tor or law - yer or In - di - an chief or hook - er or moth - er or A -

C   D7   Am   Bm

ra - bi - an sheik, The choi - ces you make are the

C   D7   G   *Fine*

choi - ces you'll see what do you do, It's up to you.

2. It's up to you what do you do?
   It's up to you what do you do?
   Old school days, relations, your job, as is
   Public places and critters will make you all sing
   The choices you make are the choices at stake
   What do you do? It's up to you.

Bridge

F / C / G

Im - ag - i - na - tion___ the look in your

C / F / C

eye is not your old cra - zies___ *Repeat 1st verse*

E / F / G

Just the world fly - ing by.

- Ask the new employer for more security.
- Keep on hunting for a day job.

3. The host goes into the audience to find out personal responses.
4. On a split screen, the studio audience and the home viewing audience are compared.
5. The expert opinion on the choice is superimposed on the screen.
6. The ensemble acts out the different solutions (resolutions)—that is, the most common audience opinion and the experts' opinion.
7. Then the next situation is enacted.

Add your basic premise for a show:

_____

_____

_____

GUIDING YOUNG PEOPLE
TO MAKE UP PLAYS

Throughout this book, ideas have been offered for those of you who will be working with children. You have just finished telling a group of children a story. There is an air of expectation in the room. The group wants to act out the tale. But are the children ready? Are you? There are, of course, many techniques for story dramatization. What follows is one that involves the use of the three Ws—*Who? What? Where?* The approach balances *planned* procedure and the children's own *spontaneity* and natural dialogue. Here's how to proceed.

ESTABLISHING THE "WHO"
Begin by selecting your cast. A good idea is to double or triple the cast and list on the board all the characters with the

names of the children portraying them. In a semicircular arrangement, the cast sits on the floor facing your "magic stage," a special space in the classroom reserved for creative drama. Once the children step onto this "stage," they are encouraged to "be" the characters by *acting* like them with both their bodies and minds.

To help the youngsters keep clear about the characters and their goals and obstacles in the story, try playing "Circle of Characters." You and the children take turns asking the character onstage various questions that establish who he or she is—including favorite color, favorite sport, age, strong desires, and so forth. For example, when we dramatized *The Emperor's New Clothes*, the title character was asked how old he was, to which he replied, "Nine." Bowing to him, I asked, "How old did you say, Emperor?" His reply now, after some obvious thought: "About thirty-three, I think."

ESTABLISHING THE "WHAT"

The character on the magic stage also has an opportunity to think about what he or she wants most in terms of the story. The emperor wants new clothes; the empress to please her husband; the swindlers to make money, etc. Characters in a dramatic presentation should also be asked what they will be doing at the beginning and conclusion of each scene. During this phase of planning, the protagonist and antagonist (or other pairs of characters) can enter the playing area at the same time and play out selected moments of conflict.

ESTABLISHING THE "WHERE"

A chair is placed in the center of the playing area. A character is asked to come to the stage, sit on a "where chair," close his or her eyes, and make a 360-degree arc, pointing out the various decor and furniture to be used in each scene: the throne, the royal exits and entrances, the king's clothes closet, the swindler's weaving room, and so forth.

The character who is most closely associated with a set (the swindlers and the weaving room, for example) should have the opportunity to describe it from the "where chair," but other children can offer suggestions for adding or deleting decor and props (mimed preferably) until the necessary number is established.

Youngsters improvise a scene from *Alice in Wonderland.*
(*Photo by Harout Merigan*)

Children should also be encouraged to think about the "when" of their play—time of day, seasonal changes in the story, and the like. Music and simple classroom lighting can serve to create a mood for both the "where" and "when," just as a simple prop or piece of clothing can serve to motivate interest and establish the "who" and "what."

After the three Ws are introduced, briefly review the sequence of key incidents; then plunge right into the play. There is a danger of *too much* discussion before the play, since the tension needed for the group creative process may be spilled. (I have found it more desirable to have the discussion flow from the actual doing.)

When the children enact the story, it may be scene by scene with evaluation coming after scene; or they may play the story right through without interruption. The first attempt may be made in pantomime to establish the story line clearly. Dialogue (improvised by the children, of course) may be added the second time around. Alternatively, the youngsters may (with some inevitable coaching on your part) play the entire story through with dialogue. If a number of casts enact the story or different children play the same character throughout one enactment, each scene will be different at each playing, because the dialogue will never be frozen by being written and memorized. Preplanning in the form of active questions and the opportunity for youngsters to act out some of the characters' key actions enhances free-flowing play in the actual dramatization. Natural dialogue and inventive business will be stimulated when the children have a reservoir of pretested ideas that can be qualitatively transformed in the process of doing.

Whether you base your play on a song from the past, today's headlines, a prop you can touch, or a dream floating in your memory, have fun making up your play and acting it out.

PLAYER'S DIARY

1. What was the play you *most* enjoyed helping to create? Why?

2. What was your *least* favorite play? Why?

3. What prop(s) triggered your Bag-O'-Drama skit? What character was likely to have this prop? How was it used in the play?

4. Did your Bag-O'-Drama skit have a conflict? How was the conflict resolved?

5. Did everyone have a part in the skit? Whose play was it (central character)? What was the central character's major goal? Who or what blocked the goal (opposing character)?

6. What kind of an audience involvement play would you like to do?

7. Would the play be any different for radio than for TV?

8. Do you have an idea for a skit? Tell who the characters are and what the idea of the skit is.

9. If you could help children make up a play, which story would you use? How would you go about helping the children prepare, plan, and play out the story?

10. Would you like to *write* a play someday? Can you briefly tell who the central character is, what he or she wants, and who the opposing character is? How is the central conflict resolved?

Add your own questions, thoughts, and observations.

I hear and I forget,
I see and I remember,
I do and I understand.

Chinese Proverb

DRAMA IN THE CLASSROOM 12

According to developmental psychologist Jean Piaget, we not only learn what we do, but we learn through what we invent. By using our dramatic imaginations to explore open-ended problems, we challenge the mind to perceive new and fresh ways of relating previously unrelated materials, movements, patterns, words, symbols, and ideas. In short, we begin to experience and live with creative changes. Change is growth, and growth is learning.

CREATIVE EXPLORATION

Too often in schools, "drilling and grilling" of facts is stressed in place of creative exploration of the meaning of those facts in relationship to the world of the learner. As Goethe observed, when interest lags, memory lags too. The assimilation, retention, and transfer of knowledge takes place more readily in a creative atmosphere, where people can become what they are learning through expanding their inner imaginations. Facts and concepts become more permanently fixed in our minds when the experience is a visceral one involving the emotions, when we can actively express feelings and get "inside" the particular subject we are studying.

Movement, nonverbal communication, and verbal improvisation help to bring creativity and personal experience into the learning process. These activities afford opportunities for participants to grow in understanding people with a different viewpoint through portraying characters and situations in history, literature, and contemporary life. You can reach a deeper understanding of people and events you have read or heard about by experiencing—through simulated play—the feelings, doubts, aspirations, and beliefs of characters from past, present, and future.

The creative use of dramatic improvisation, if nothing else, motivates and stimulates people to connect their own feelings with the subjects they are studying, so that material becomes alive and exciting.

For example, Carl Sandburg's whimsical poem "Arithmetic" vividly conveys the elasticity and excitement of numbers when they "fly like pigeons in and out of your head." Such a statement can become even more meaningful for students if they themselves become the birds flying in and out of a circle to illustrate the concepts of addition and subtraction. In this way, things learned in school are not "subjects" but expressions of creative activity.

ART PROJECTS

SPACE-DRAWING
Write your name in space using both your arms (or whole body) as a brush. Next, lie on the floor, using your legs as the

brush. What have you discovered about your own name that you didn't know before?

DISCOVER SHAPES, LINES, LEVELS, AND INTERSECTIONS

Individually, find these shapes with your own body:

flat	elliptical
round	oblong
open	long
closed	jagged

In pairs, find the following shapes or forms:

parallels	closed figures
intersections	circles
semicircles	open figures
diamonds	crossovers

In groups, make moving

parallelograms	octagons
stars	rectangles
circles	cubes

Add your own:

_____ _____

_____ _____

_____ _____

1. Make a straight *line* with one part of your body, then with your whole body.

2. Move in straight lines. Make a zigzag with your body. (Note that a zigzag is composed of straight lines.)

3. Make a *curve* with your body. What is a curve composed of? Move in curves around the room.

4. Make *right angles* with your body. What are they composed of? Move in right angles around the room as if in a busy subway station or bus depot. Try not to bump into anyone.

233

Players discover lines and shapes.
(*Photo by Tom Fridy*)

5. Tell a simple visual story in pantomime, adding sounds if you like; each player adds one significant movement.

6. Try the story in zigzag movements, right angles, and curves. Incorporate different *levels*—high, medium, and low. A conductor can control the intersections.

7. After having these experiences, draw your impressions of the scenes incorporating a variety of lines, levels, and shapes. You may wish to verbalize your feelings after expressing them through drawings.

SCULPTURE AND CLAY

1. How many different ways can you bend your body? How does this affect the space around you? Experiment with movable sculpture and mobiles in groups.

2. Explore a bagful of props of all kinds. How does it feel to touch something warm, cold, rough, smooth, hard, soggy, spongy, or what? Become the objects. Describe the different textures. Mold them with real clay. Let your imagination run wild. "Clacting" is what I call the dynamic combination of

The children put acting and working with clay together—clacting.

(*Photos by Harout Merigan*)

acting and working with clay. This amalgamation of clay and play can be very stimulating as players act out different kinds of appliances, machines, animals, and toys they have created in mime and then mold them out of clay.

COLORS

1. Act out your favorite colors. Why are they your favorites—what is the *personal* association? Act out warm colors, cool colors, and their combinations. Become a sunflower or morning glory, and then paint your impressions. Take a trip to the bottom of the sea, and explore treasures, pearls, ocean rocks. (You might encounter a people-eating shark, so be careful!) Express your visual impressions with colored chalk so as to obtain a "soft" effect for the ocean atmosphere. Act out a scene with a theme (e.g., "Family Tree" or "Space Age"). Express your interpretations using crayons, colored pencils, or chalk. Explore *color connotations*. What does red mean to you? Act out your impressions (hot, vibrant, dangerous, sexy, etc.). Green? White? Black? Purple? Make an association with *one* color, and act it out individually and/or in groups (e.g., green-eyed monster, feeling blue, red with rage, and so on).

2. Divide into two teams, each one dramatizing a mood of a color, and try to convey its *essence* to the other team.

3. What *objects* and *places* are associated with color (school walls, hospital rooms, dance halls, and so forth)?

4. Hold a "conversation in mime" between two colors. Now add speech. Combine colors, taking into consideration hues, shades, and saturation. For example, a shady, envious green pitcher tries to expel a sun-drenched orange punch drink.

5. Make a still life with objects of your choice.

GROUP MURAL

Your group may wish to experiment with making a mural of a city, country, or sea scene after enacting the objects and the people. For example, what would happen if your city or town were suddenly to come alive? How does the group feel about carrying so many buildings, becoming dirty, polluted, and noisy? What good points about the city or town emerged through enactment, and how can these advantages be communicated in the artwork? For a maritime scene, how does the wind cause your boat to be propelled across the lake? With hands over head and bodies bending from side to side, the players become the billowing sails, and the sails become part of the person.

ART APPRECIATION

Acting out a painting enables one to appreciate better the artist, the circumstances under which the painting was made, and the background of the work. Any number of improvisational techniques already discussed can be applied to appreciating the content of famous and not-so-famous paintings. Think of some activity mime to create images of what you think da Vinci's *Mona Lisa* or Modigliani's *Girl with Braids* would do if she were to come alive. Phylis Boksen's students in New York acted out a group improvisation contrasting *The Artist's Mother* by Albrecht Dürer and *Whistler's Mother*. Enact a sono-mime (Chapter 7) to suggest what *The Knight, Death and the Devil* by Dürer are doing. Do the mirror game (Chapter 3) to perceive how *The Artist in His Studio* (Rembrandt) perceives himself. Create in mime the objects in Chardin's *Kitchen Still Life*. Make a machine to explore the feelings of *The Three Musicians* by Pablo Picasso. Take any expressive painting, such as *The Wheat Field with Cypresses* by Van Gogh, and capture what you feel is its mood in movement and pantomime. How do you feel running .barefoot through the wheat fields? Can you feel the warmth of the sun in your hair and the breeze blowing through the trees? Now use some of these same techniques to explore paintings that you and your friends have made.

CURRENT EVENTS

CONTEMPORARY CLIPPINGS

1. Scan the newspaper for a headline, article, item, or picture that vitally interests the class—something you care about deeply.

2. The class reads the item carefully and discusses what took place, using as a guide *who* you are, *what* you want, *where* you are, and *when* the action takes place.

3. List key characters and places mentioned in the story.

4. Ask for volunteers for all roles.

5. Act out the situation, following the incident fairly closely.

6. After acting out the incident as it really happened, ask the students how they might have reacted as the characters in a similar situation. In discussion, consider the technique of valuing, a process that involves making choices and decisions. In the valuing process, consider the nature, worth, and dignity of humanity at its best and worst and all the gradations in between. Is there meaning and value to life? What values are esteemed by the group?

7. After discussing their own reactions, class members are ready to do the improvisation again. This time, however, students should feel free to alter the facts and play the scene as they feel they would have responded.

8. As an alternative, act out a courtroom trial of the original incident. Involve the whole class. Shyer students can play members of the jury—or perhaps the judge! Stress making the courtroom scene believable and all the characters real. List the

Dr. Martin Luther King, Jr. receives the Nobel Peace Prize as part of Brotherhood Week Happening at P.S. 50.
(*Photo by Steve Denes*)

roles and their responsibilities on the board, and clarify court-room procedures. Have fun turning your "Classroom into a Courtroom."

LANGUAGE ARTS

Acting out words in an enjoyable atmosphere helps to enlarge both listening and speaking vocabularies, as well as reading and writing skills. The concentration needed for looking and listening helps young people to be alert and to sense the importance of having the right words available to express themselves. They become more keenly aware of what can be said with words and what can be communicated silently. Pantomiming words and sentences helps us understand concepts better. For example, contrast the prepositions *in* and *out* by enacting this rhyme: "We plant a seed in the soil, so that a flower grows/Then we sprinkle water/Which comes out of a hose." Or contrast words that sound alike: First pantomime taking some *clothes* from the closet; then *close* the closet door. Now write the two words on the blackboard, and note differences in spellings.

To connect the world of language arts and pantomime artists, refer to the enticing *Marcel Marceau Alphabet Book*, which contains delightful photographs of Marcel in his Bip costume awakening to meet the new day for the letter A, bending down to pick an imaginary flower for F, striking the attitude of happiness for H, etc. Imagine him trying to make the Chinese alphabet, which consists of over two thousand letters! Reading abilities are improved when children can identify with characters they become a part of through participating in a story or poem. Written expression, in turn, is enhanced by having something to say that flows from being emotionally involved with the content.

WORD PLAY

When words are made physical, their meaning becomes more apparent. The leader calls out a variety of words

spongy	fantastic
supercilious	frilly
amiable	fudgey

Add your own:

_____   _____

_____   _____

_____   _____

The players move to them, capturing how they *feel* about the words. The leader then extends the vocabulary by contrasting one word with another word (e.g., rhyming *frilly* with *silly*). Participants can then talk about or write their impressions of word meanings.

MAKING LETTERS WITH THE BODY

The class is randomly divided into several teams of four or five players. The leader calls out a letter. The team that makes

Bodies make letters: T-I-P to P-I-T to T-O-P.
(Photo courtesy of Lou Esposito)

a letter (capital or small) correctly in the shortest amount of time receives a point. The variations of this game are endless. For example, the class can be divided into subgroups of five players each. Each group thinks of a five-letter word and makes the word with their bodies. Groups can then form a simple sentence. In groups of three players each, letters can be rearranged to make different words, changing, for example, B-I-G to B-A-G or C-A-T to C-O-T, or placing letters backwards to form opposite concepts such as T-I-P to P-I-T, P-O-T to T-O-P.

ABC POTPOURRI

One game begins: "My ship (or plane, boat, train, etc.) is loaded with a _____ (something beginning with A)." The game continues with players going through the alphabet and pantomiming the objects in a simple action mime. Another alphabet game: Pick an object, and assign to it an adjective, which is then enacted. For example:

- average box
- battered box
- cool box

Add your own:

d_____ box
e_____ box
f_____ box
g_____ box
h_____ box

MIMES THAT RHYME: GUESSING GAMES

The leader stands inside a circle formation and says, "I'm thinking of something that rhymes with _____." This should be a short, one-syllable word, such as *bat, shoe, car,* etc. For example, the leader has chosen the word *key* and says, "I'm thinking of a word that rhymes with *tea.*" The other players, one at a time, pantomime what they think is the correct word. The player who guesses the word goes into the middle of the circle and thinks of another word, and the game continues.

THREE-WAY

Three words are given to a group of three people, who enact a skit involving the three words.

DEFINITIONS

In groups, players act out the meaning of a word, using action and fantasy mime.

SHARE-A-STORY

A group starts out with some basic vocabulary words, and each one in the circle continues telling the story using one of the vocabulary words. As a guideline, all the players should remember *who* they are, *what* they are doing, and *where* they are.

Add your own:

_____

_____

_____

Nursery rhymes and limericks such as "Jack and Jill," "Jack Be Nimble," "Little Bo Peep," and "Little Tommy Tucker" are fun to act out. Individuals or a group of players can serve as narrators, or players can take turns being the narrator and performers at different times. Nursery rhymes can also be enacted, with different verses appearing in reverse order or in other scrambled positions.

FIRST AND LAST

Pantomime can also be combined with writing skills in the following way. The first and last letters of a word are written on the board, such as a ___ ___ ___ c. The player who has an idea of what the word is enters the rest of the letters in the spaces provided and then pantomimes it—in this case, perhaps walking upstairs, opening the door, and rummaging around the *attic.*

PANTOMIME SENTENCES

In this variation of machines, the leader calls out specific words comprising a sentence, and the players arrange themselves in the correct order with the appropriate action. For example:

> ran   today   the   slowly   bear   cave   to   the
> (The bear ran slowly to the cave today.)

In this way, students learn the proper placement of nouns, verbs, and prepositions while having creative fun.

During miming, inner dialogue is continually going on within each player to complement the visual vocabulary that is unfolding to paint body pictures in space. What is magically occurring is alertness through a keen sense of *active* listening and observing what the other players are becoming. No one speaks; the concentration becomes so intensified that one can almost see it on the faces and bodies in the room. Observation and active listening, so important for language development, are encouraged and fostered.

It sometimes defies imagination to witness how a noisy classroom can be transformed into lovely realms of silence, wherein people are acutely tuned in to each other's feelings, where they develop inner controls, daring not to impose upon someone else's silent world—especially when engaged in a similar kind of creation. Because we are bombarded daily with so many devastating levels of noise, it is refreshing, indeed, to be able to savor hearing our inner worlds of silence from time to time.

MUSIC

The creative teacher looks for opportunities to integrate classroom subjects into a meaningful whole, so that variegated aspects of the human experience become interrelated. For example, the rhythmic game "Ten Little Indians" combines math, music, and storytelling. Acting out children's songs,

243

such as "Old McDonald Had a Farm," and nursery rhymes helps young children, in turn, to become familiar with their bodies and to express themselves while enjoying the creative contributions of their classmates. With Haydn's *Clock* and *Toy* Symphonies, children can express the music with their bodies by becoming the penny trumpet, whistle, and little drum, or they can imagine that they are playing these toy instruments.

Whenever possible, students should have opportunities to dance, mime, or move to different moods of various recordings. For example, to Beethoven's *Pastoral Symphony*, they can portray different rustic moods. The first movement can be used to create a winter scene, with participants skating, sleigh riding, throwing snowballs. Another movement portrays a spring scene, offering contrast for pantomimic moods. With Stravinsky's *Firebird Suite* playing in the background, children (individually or in groups) can become the sun rising, the bird, and other suggested images. Thus, appreciation for music is

Making the notes helps the children to feel them.
(*Photo courtesy of Performing Arts Foundation of Long Island*)

DRAMA IN THE CLASSROOM

enhanced because it has touched the nervous system and has been kinesthetically expressed.

In explaining abstract concepts such as scales, the process should be made physical. Children can become the notes themselves, jumping up and down in various rhythms and durations. A simple song such as "Hot Cross Buns," for example, has only three tones, with one player for each tone in a line: one squatting, one standing, and one standing on a chair—all showing the rise and fall of the melody.

SYMPHONIC SOUNDS

An orchestra can be formed with a conductor and players pantomiming the different instruments. Sounds can be added, with the percussion section setting the basic rhythm for the group and the conductor cuing in the various instruments. The players can become the instruments themselves. For example, the tuba player blows himself up with a big fat belly, eyes bulging, and a big, vibrating, brass sound. The piano sways back and forth with her double row of black and white keys. The two-person bass plucks his or her own strings, or another player becomes a bow and moves across the strings. A player moves the folds of an accordian made by the body movements of two players. Combinations of players can be musicians and instruments.

MUSIC HISTORY

Any number of techniques can be applied to studying different periods of music history—from Bach to Basin Street to the Beatles and beyond. For example, players can make a time machine and go back to Bach and the Baroque period. Take your time machine back to any period, or visit composers working today. If you are in the Classical period, sono-mime interview the child genius Mozart concerning his opinions of music today.

Add your own:

_____

_____

_____

SCIENCE

What better way to explore and discover the process of scientific inquiry than through dramatic play. Both scientific and dramatic discovery involve an open mind, flexibility, originality, skepticism, persistence, elaboration, and the ability to deal with the forces of conflict. It takes the ability to see and observe, concentration, self-confidence, and a playful intellect to come up with diverse solutions to a nagging problem. Improvisation enables students to become adventurous explorers, to share the peaks of elation and depths of despair that men and women of science have experienced in their quest for knowledge about ourselves and our environment. Indeed, youngsters and oldsters alike enjoy discussing and comparing the processes that scientists and creative artists (themselves) have in common: The groping in the dark and facing the unknown; the role of observable evidence and intuition, our sixth sense; the gnawing periods of false starts and trial and error; the need for preparation, involving both conscious deliberation and spontaneous improvisation in which a "constructive accident" sometimes triggers new dimensions of discovery; the flash or insight where the ends and means of problem solving come together; the periods of revision and testing the hunch that originally stimulated the inquiry; and more testing—searching, selecting, starting anew, vision, and revision. Through improvisation, young people become drama detectives and search for scientific clues and evidence in nature and natural forces.

SCENES FROM SCIENTIFIC DISCOVERY

Recreate the discovery of fire, the invention of the wheel and the knife, the discovery of oxygen, and so forth. Contrast scenes of alchemy with modern science. Transform into various objects—a jagged rock in time becoming a lump of clay. How did your transformation take place? How did you move then, and how do you move now? What did you do differently then and now? How did the sun and wind and rain affect your transformation? Show us. What are the properties of fire? Show with your body how these properties transform themselves and what happens when metals such as copper are af-

Compare the two types of thermometers—fever and weather—through discussion, demonstration, and dramatization.

(Photo by Ken Korsh, courtesy of Performing Arts Foundation of Long Island)

fected by fire. Compare two types of thermometers—fever and weather—through discussion, demonstration, and dramatization. With the latter, for example, players volunteer to act out seasonal activities and correlate them with the rising or lowering of mercury. If the players are outdoors swimming, the mercury goes up; it goes down when they are ice-skating. You can discuss the boiling and freezing points on the thermometer and devise activities to illuminate those concepts. Capture the steps leading to the moment of such discoveries as the microscope, the telescope, penicillin, antipolio vaccine. Discuss what forces and social climates led and contributed to the discoveries you have dramatized.

EXPLORING CONCEPTS

Abstract concepts in the physical and life sciences can be made more concrete for students through dramatic play. When studying biology, students can make a Photosynthesis Machine to get a better grasp of the relationship of elements that make plants grow. A Body Building Machine can be made to facilitate the comprehension of the nature of metabolism: proteins to build carbohydrates for energy, fats for fuel, water for digestion, minerals for strong bones, and vitamins to regulate life and growth. This can be followed by group discussion and perhaps a story about plants (such as Glenn Blough's *Wait for Sunshine*) showing how they live and grow and the role sunshine and the seasons play in their growth. This can be followed by a dramatization of flowers in different stages of growth. It is fun to take a journey through the body, becoming the bloodstream, blood cells, muscle fibers, and the like. Play a variation of "Streets and Alleys," called "Arteries and Veins," where conflict situations (such as red blood cells being engulfed by white blood cells) are enacted.

Concepts of floating and sinking can be discovered by imagining that the body is a box filled with sand and dumped into water. The box can be slowly transformed into a submarine with air holes. First the players float; when the air holes become filled with water, they begin to submerge. The players can then experiment with other floating and sinking objects.

Nursing students study different kinds of bones by simulating them with their bodies.

(*Photo by Harout Merigan*)

To discover the components of electricity, they can become live circuits, telegraph units, pop-up toasters, and the like.

Add your own:

_____

_____

_____

STUDYING THE SOLAR SYSTEM

One good way to motivate youngsters to investigate the solar system is to have them become astronauts. To prepare the junior space travelers, here are some creative adaptations:

ASTRONAUT'S TRAINING

Vibrating Machine. Designed to simulate vibrations caused by machinery operating in a vehicle as well as possible barriers in the atmosphere.

Gravity. Trainees practice spinning around in a giant centrifuge; they sit on seats inside metal cylinders and spin around while velocity increases.

*Weightlessness.*The exercises done in an airplane flow up and down in parabolic arcs. When the arc is at a certain point, there is a thirty-second sensation of weightlessness.

Who Am I? Trainees are asked to compose quickly a long list of words that

IMPROVISATIONAL ADAPTATION

Players bounce up and down first with "heavy" shoes, then "light" ones; other "in-place" exercises for warm-ups.

Players practice rotating their whole bodies (legs too!). They loosen up head, neck, and back muscles.

Each player or group is asked to imagine for thirty seconds being a feather or piece of paper floating down, the wind, and so on.

Flight director takes down the players' lists. Each player is asked to panto-

ASTRONAUT'S TRAINING	IMPROVISATIONAL ADAPTATION
describe their own individual personalities.	mime an activity conditioned by one word that describes his or her personality.
Gravitational Pull. A 180-pound person appears to have a weight of 1½ tons during gravitational pull.	After a discussion of gravity, each player acts out the feeling of extreme heaviness—a toppling building, an elephant, and so on.
Heat Chamber. To measure trainees' ability to perform decision-making tasks under high thermal loads, temperature is raised to 135° Fahrenheit.	*Problem:* It is the hottest day of your life. Act out different ways of beating the heat.
Isolation. Trainees are locked in a lightproof, soundproof room for as long as they can hold out.	*Problem:* You have been punished and must remain all alone in your room. Act out your feelings.

Add your own:

_____	_____
_____	_____
_____	_____

Now we are ready for a trip around the solar system to check out gravity and make explorations. Youngsters put on their spacesuits, helmets, oxygen tanks, and space shoes. Take your time. Do it right, for the rest of the world is watching on TV. Don't forget the packaged breakfasts and Tang—you will need all the energy you can get. Countdown:—10–9–8–7–6–5–4–3–2–1—Blast Off! Everything looks so small as we soar off. One good dramatic in-flight game is a variation of Statues and Swingers: Astronauts and Copilots. An astronaut hurls his or her copilot into space, where the copilot is frozen by the cold stratosphere. The copilot can only be unfrozen when his or her partner starts to pantomime some action that is based on the position the copilot assumed after being hurled. The copilot must guess the partner's action, which involves some familiar "earthly" action, before continuing the trip.

Another way to visit other planets and explore and discover salient facts about the solar system is to make a Time Machine. For example, let's visit Mercury, the smallest planet nearest to the sun. One side always faces the sun and is hot and bright, and the other side is always cold and dark. Youngsters can keep moving from one side to the other, experiencing alternating sensations of hot and cold. They can pretend to eat a space ice cream cone that will melt on the warm side and freeze on the cold side.

SOCIAL STUDIES

Creative improvisation is concerned with expression and communication that extends to social relationships of all sorts. For example, making a farm and portraying animals and stimulating the agricultural process helps city dwellers to understand country living better. The rural inhabitant, in turn, is fascinated by towering buildings, crowded subway scenes, busy streets, and other aspects of city living. Nearly everyone loves to discover processes and how things work. This interest can be combined with recreating the jobs of mail personnel, hospital workers, bakers, and so on.

HISTORICAL SCENES

Historical scenes that involve action are fun to recreate through improvisation. These include such landmarks as the signing of the Magna Carta, Columbus sailing for the East and discovering America, the role-playing of Indians and pioneers. When studying American history, improvisations involving conflict will stimulate interest in the past and present problems: One student is a colonial farmer; another, a merchant living in New York. They are arguing about who is contributing more to the country. Show what they do. What things did early craftspeople in this country produce? Show us. What is the role of the artist today? Add as many characters (patrons, government, and so on) as will bring the scene alive.

PANTOMIME PRESS CONFERENCE

In sono-mime (Chapter 7), recreate dramatic debates between historical personalities such as Christ and Pontius Pilate; Socrates and his accusers; Galileo and his disbelievers; Martin Luther King in a Birmingham jail or in the March on Washington; and Sojourner Truth speaking out for women's rights. Players should make their points in the strongest and clearest way possible.

TAKE A TRIP

Take an imaginary trip around a country, acting out something specially identified with it—for example, making lace in Belgium, cutting diamonds in Holland, making clocks in Switzerland. It is fun and instructive to make shapes of countries and states with the body and construct a Human Globe or map with one or more bodies. This fosters appreciation of size, terrain, and distance.

COMPARE CUSTOMS AND LIFE-STYLES

Take a trip to foreign lands such as Africa, England, China, and Puerto Rico; explore different customs and ways of life. Whenever possible, learn dances native to the country, such as the Russian Korobushka, the German Children's Polka, Scandinavian Wooden Shoes, and the Hungarian Csehbogar. Whenever feasible, adapt games and stories indigenous to the country. For example, while in Puerto Rico, play "La Cebolli" (the little onion). One player is the seller; another, the buyer; the rest are the onions.

NATURAL PHENOMENA

Working in groups, capture the essence of a flood, tornado, earthquake, avalanche. What do these natural phenomena have in common? In what ways are they different from one another?

INTERFERENCE

Divide into two groups. The first group becomes natural elements such as a garden, the ocean, a forest, and so on. The second group becomes elements that will pollute the creations of the first group. Afterward discuss the teams' creative efforts.

MAKE MACHINES

Make a Survival Machine (Chapter 4), capturing with sounds and body motion the various noises of survival—the bark of a dog, the crying of a baby just born, etc. Make a Harmony Machine showing how nature and people can work together to solve the pollution problem. Make a Recycling Machine, and discuss its components. Devise a skit about survival and nuclear power.

CREATE-A-WORLD OF MANY COUNTRIES

Variation of Create-a-World (Chapter 8). A player acts out the essence of each country in pantomime; a new player joins in and changes the essence of the country. For example, in Create-a-World of Switzerland, Player 1 might go into the circle and mime climbing the Alps; Player 2 might make watches; Player 3 might create the world of commerce or some aspect of culture. In the skits, combine the media of music, art, and dance to complement the dramatic activity.

Add your own:

_____

_____

_____

CLASSROOM OR
ASSEMBLY HAPPENINGS

EXAMPLES OF THEME: THE CREATION

1. Warm-Up: The void (Yoga, Stream of Sand, Chapter 3; Blind Walk, Chapter 2; Creation Machine, Chapter 4).

2. Man and woman discover each other (Mirrors, Chapter 4; Trust Exercise, Chapter 2).

3. Humans discover animals (Machines, Chapter 4; Transformations and Fantasy Mime, Chapter 6 & 7).

4. Humans discover language (Gibberish, Chapter 5).

5. Humans discover socialization (Sono-mime, Chapter 7) and role-playing (Chapter 10).

PLANNING THE HAPPENING

1. Structures should be simple enough to allow spontaneity to develop. For example, when creating a "Friend-Ship" for a St. Valentine Day Love-In, the simple direction to form a ship on the floor in mime is all that is necessary.

2. There should be transitions from one activity unit to another to ensure a logical flow. For example, during a Winter Magic Happening, children going through a Toy Machine came out as their favorite toys; the "toys" were then rounded up and taken to a department store, where they came alive at the stroke of midnight and went into a "dance of toys."

3. The event should allow for variety of rhythm and pacing, with more passive, simple pantomime alternating with greater action and movement (e.g., making machines followed by the Magic Scarf game, Chapter 8).

4. There should be one leader or director of the happening who acts as coordinator. Activities within the happening should be led by various students.

5. Ask for volunteers for the committees: decorations, publicity, invitations, and so on (see Appendix B).

Add your own:

_____

_____

_____

A combination of drama and a variety of school subjects not only help to revitalize what is being studied but give freshness and additional insight into the art of communication. Li Li-

Weng, a Chinese philosopher of the seventeenth century, observed: "First we see the hills in the painting, and then we see the painting in the hills." In improvisational play, dramatic activity and cognitive areas often blend into a wonderful whole.

PLAYER'S DIARY

1. In what ways does art come alive through drama and other creative expression?

2. What is your favorite painting? Can you express the feeling it has for you through improvisation?

3. What event from history or today's headlines has left the greatest impact on you? Why? Can you describe this event nonverbally by yourself or with others? Verbally?

4. How do you feel about pollution and the destruction of the land? What can you *do* about it? Can you act out some possible solutions?

5. If you could visit any place in the world, where would it be? Why? Can you show—through your body and gestures—what place this would be?

6. If you could take a Time Machine back to any period in history, what would it be? Why? Can you show what historical period it would be through improvisation?

7. Why is nonverbal expression and communication important in language arts? How can you show that nonverbal communication is a language of its own?

8. How are music and drama related? Can you show this?

9. How are the scientific and artistic processes related? Can you show the relationship?

10. What is your favorite exercise or activity in this chapter? Why?

Add your own questions, thoughts, and observations.

SHADOWS AND STORIES 13

Our concluding dramatic activities can be equally effective in the classroom or onstage. In the first activity you will explore the exciting mixed media of shadows. In the second activity you will tell stories, not only verbally but with your body as well.

SHADOW THEATER

A surefire activity to spark your dramatic imagination is shadow theater. Shadow plays as entertainment originated in the Orient two thousand years ago and are still popular in every Eastern country.

In addition to learning about a fascinating theater form and integrating this form with the media of art, dance, music, and photography, one can gain other important benefits from shadow theater. It is an excellent technique for dealing with the shy or less experienced improvisational player, because the shadow screen that comes between the actors and the audience greatly reduces feelings of self-consciousness and stage fright.

Shadow players can act out situations, skits, and even whole plays using cardboard puppets or human bodies or combinations of the two to produce shadows. You might recall from camp days those wild Dr. Kronkite skits in which all kinds of fanciful things—saws, tubing, clocks, you name it—were extracted from the body of an unfortunate patient being operated on (behind a shadow screen, of course). You will also recall that the challenge in those skits consisted of drawing from the richness of imagination and not on costly props. The trick of shadow play is not how the prop or character appears in daylight but in shadow. Thus in shadow, a belt will be perfect as a rare snake. Some doweling will serve fine as a telescope; an old sweater will simulate the appearance of the costliest cape. The effect is the important thing, not how it is achieved.

Now let us go into greater detail about the equipment you will need, at the same time taking a brief historical excursion across the shadows of time.

THE SCREEN

In Chinese shadow theater, whether performed in palaces or villages, mulberry screens were often used; in India the screens were sometimes made of beautiful white saris.

Any transparent flat surface will do as a shadow screen as long as the material is transparent enough for the shadows to show through the opposite side. Any of the following materials will make a good screen: a white cotton bed sheet for casting human shadows, an old white (but clean!) window shade or tracing paper for a smaller puppet screen. Groups I have worked with have tacked a window shade or bed sheet across an open classroom doorway with satisfactory results. Regardless of the type of screen or sheet used, it is important to mask the sides and bottom to conceal the operators and to focus light properly on the screen.

For improvisational shadow play, it is important to remember that the characters need most of the screen space in which to move; so the scenery should be minimal, preferably merely suggested. One or two side pieces can frame the center of the acting area. Some scenery can be painted later (a felt-tipped marker will do). Black cardboard or construction paper can be pinned on the screen to indicate mountains, rivers, or far-off places. Small pieces of scenery (such as a fire that goes out and then reappears) may be propped in place with a control rod or manipulated by means of a pulley string pinned on the screen. Simple scenery can be projected onto the screen by drawing or painting realistic or abstract figures on clear or colored gelatin or X-ray sheeting and placing them on an overhead projector.

LIGHT SOURCE

In the ancient Chinese shows, as Bill Severn relates, lighting was produced by means of a torch, which might sometimes accidentally set the whole show in flames.*

A single 150–200-watt bulb placed approximately four to six feet behind the screen provides an adequate light source for a screen 7 feet by 12 feet. Make sure the bulb is high enough to eliminate the operator's shadow. For a smaller screen or table screen, a small table lamp or high-intensity light is fine. In determining the exact distance and position of your light source, it is always a good idea to experiment. Once, when we were doing a Hunter Halloween Happening that required shadow play, to our utter horror, all the lighting outlets went on the blink. However, a thin crack of light appearing through a covered window gave off the right intensity. *Make sure any and all lighting setups are absolutely fireproof.*

Colored lighting can be effected by placing sheets of gelatin or colored slides in front of the light source at different times. A blue gel, for example, evokes a nocturnal scene and

* Bill Severn, *Shadow Magic* (New York: D. McKay, 1959), p.103.

Dazzling effects can be obtained by working with two or three overhead projections.
(Photo by Terry Buchalter)

pink, early morning. Complementary coloring should be observed; that is, a red light interrupted by the figure will throw off a green shadow. Dazzling effects can be achieved by experimenting with two or three overhead projections, each of which is covered by a different-colored plastic gel. Start with the primary colors—red, green, and blue—and add and eliminate the gels from projectors. One human figure behind the screen will appear in multicolored images. A truly technicolor delight!

WARM-UP EXERCISES WITH HUMAN SHADOWS

1. One or two students can mime-dance to a few minutes of evocative music.

2. Play the mirror game in shadow, either in color or black and white.

Build a Human Shadow Machine.
(Photo by Terry Buchalter)

3. Construct a Human Shadow Machine, either in color or black and white.

4. Move or act out poetry behind the screen. Haiku poetry is especially effective. A haiku has sixteen or seventeen syllables and is unrhymed. Time is almost frozen yet fluid, as resplendent nature is joined with human nature. For example, high-school student Cathy Toscano composed the following haiku:

> *The bare*
> *Tree*
> *Stands cold;*
> *The last bird has left*
> *Its branch*
> *Alone against wind.*

5. Enact action pantomimes, fantasy mimes, or sono-mimes, picking flowers, playing, becoming an instrument, and so forth. You can isolate one part of the body and concentrate on it—for example, coming up with different symbols suggested by hands: peace, right on, victory, and so on.

1. The world of work and play.

2. Living and nonliving things in comparison (combine shadow puppets and live actors).

3. Take a trip (back into history or into the future).

4. Origins—the reasons for seasons, how the woodpecker got its beak, how the sun and moon came into being.

5. School gym transformed into a beautiful world, a strange world, and so forth.

6. Make a shadow monster! The first player makes a shadow with a distinct sound. Player 2 joins the first player, adding new sound and changing form to include self. Add two or three more players.

PUPPET FIGURES

The skins of donkeys and buffalo, pared down to thin parchment, provided the coverings for flat Chinese puppets. In Javanese shadow shows, which sometimes began at dusk and ended at dawn, the figures were painted with red—designating strength—or black—symbolizing restraint. The figures' jointed parts were controlled by the busy Dalang, who was the player, speaker, and singer all at once. In Siam, the puppets were perforated with hundreds of holes, adding beautifully textured images.*

For improvisational purposes, the shadow puppet figure can be made from a variety of materials. Oak tag, poster board, and other thin, stiff cardboard are excellent for casting dark shadows. Black construction paper is suitable for introductory purposes.

Remember, a good shadow play relies on the effect of the moving shape on the screen. Shadow figures are most effective when the puppets are shown from the side, in *profile.* Because it is important to have clear, distinct shadows, you must press the figure *close* to the screen.

* *Ibid.*, p. 107.

It's only a paper moon . . . and the house . . . and the witch's hat.
(*Photo by Terry Buchalter*)

For colored shadow forms, use translucent materials. Most arts and crafts supply stores stock suitable colored gelatins. Deceptively simple and fascinating color effects can be obtained by pasting colored cellophane or candy wrappings over slits in the cardboard figures. Perforated puppets are good variants, too, and you can easily make them with a small hole puncher.

Through history, many shadow puppets have been articulated with movable limbs. However, for our purposes, simpler techniques can be used. For example, the rods used to manipulate shadow puppets may be made from a wire coat hanger (straighten it out, and bend its end at a right angle; then fasten to the flat puppet with adhesive tape), long twigs or branches, wire, bicycle spokes, or umbrella ribs. The rods should be long enough to allow the operators to stand behind the light source (if it is on a table or chair behind the screen); otherwise, their bodies will show up in shadow too. Brass fasteners can also be used to hold together figures with movable parts.

SUBJECTS FOR SHADOWS

Because you are dealing with shadows, search for material containing elements of mystery and fantasy—nursery rhymes, mood poetry (such as Lewis Carroll's *Jabberwocky*), and fables. (Remember the dog who searched for his reflection in a pond and lost the substance—the meat he greedily held in his mouth?) Myths, folktales, and fairy tales are also excellent sources of dramatizations for cutout shadow plays.

Think of all the wonderful transformations players can perform with shadows. As one player remarked: "The picture language of shadows can really mysteriously relate what speech alone cannot." For changing animals into humans and vice versa, you merely pull back one puppet and push another one forward in its place. In a magic transformation, one student made a rabbit (his hand) appear as though it were coming out of a hat (made from black construction paper). In my shadow play, *The Fire Keepers*, a grey bird swoops down to prevent a fire from going out and, in the process, scorches her breast. A bird with a red cellophane insert is quickly substituted, and the robin is created in a smooth transformation. Changing little people into giants and other shrinking and growing phenomena are also easily effected.

In the dramatization of Aesop's fables, hand shadows can represent all kinds of animals and birds. Biblical tales such as *Joseph and His Brethren, Jonah and the Whale,* or *Noah's Flood* also lend themselves to shadow treatment.

You may wish to improvise situations from scripted plays, say by Ionesco or Yeats. A number of playwrights, from William Shakespeare to Tennessee Williams, have alluded to shadows. Who can forget, for example, Richard II's poignant lines: "And these external manners of laments/Are merely shadows to the unseen grief, That swells with silence in the tortured soul; There lies the substance. . . ." In Tennessee Williams's *The Glass Menagerie*, the gentleman caller's shadow stretches ominously across the ceiling minutes before he bumps into Laura's glass animals. Ben Jonson concludes his *Tale of a Tub* with a shadow puppet play in five scenes presented behind a transparent curtain.

Many historical and biographical events adapt well to

Shadow scene—Adam, Eve, and the serpent.
(*Photo by Terry Buchalter*)

shadows. You may wish to conduct shadow interviews with famous personalities from past and present. For example, two human bodies could represent Lincoln (with tall hat and beard made of black paper) confronting Douglas (with protruding finger in exaggerated stance), each on one side of the shadow screen. Philosophical concepts, such as Plato's idealistic shadow cave, and skits involving the ancient basic elements of fire, water, earth, and air can also be created.

Do not overlook original situations in which you can invent characters of your own. As a starter, you can improvise characters and situations by tearing off different shapes and sizes of cardboard. Do an improvisation between a circle and a square or between a triangle and a star ("Of course I'm better, darling—I'm in the movies"). Put a regular shoe and a platform shoe on two different hangers, and let them argue over their respective merits. In one of the skits, a giant star monster (made from human shadow players) ate up a galaxy of smaller stars until it became so bloated that it finally burst into an array of colored shooting stars (cut from construction paper and thrown onto the screen). The possibilities are endless. Let the situation grow even as the shadows grow.

Another effective application of the shadow medium is to act out your fantasies and dreams. Why not create a shadowindow to look into your dreams? In the Chinese shadow play, music was supplied by drums and cymbals; here, live or recorded music (such as the Beatles' "Magical Mystery Tour") can accompany the presentation.

In a brief planning period, the pairs of players determine their characters' main traits, chief problems, goals, and obstacles. An agreed-upon conflict is established, and the rest of the skit is improvised on the spot. Sometimes the groups consist of four players each, and the skit is enacted in sono-mime (two actors do shadow mime behind the screen while two other actors beside the screen become their voices).

PUTTING IT ALL TOGETHER

The evolution of a longer improvised play might go something like this:

WARM-UP
The players first freely experiment with shadows—both cutout and human. For human shadows, the participants make themselves grow or shrink simply by walking close to or away from the sheet or by stepping (gingerly!) over the light, thereby creating the illusion of a giant.

CREATION OF CHARACTERS AND SITUATIONS
These usually evolve through experimentation and trial and error. Always be aware of the "constructive accident" that might trigger off plot situations. For example, one player doing an improvisation with a cutout star got the idea of doing a

space shadow show. The group decided to devise an interme-dia show featuring music, cutout puppets, and humans. They decided on a conflict that builds to a satisfying dramatic cli-max. A futuristic family is watching television. The father wants to listen to the intergalactic weather report to see if he can go to the planet Pluto in the morning, but each of his children wants to watch his or her favorite space show. There is a lot of switching different television programs off and on (all in shadow) while the family assembled before the screen argues back and forth. Finally, out of desperation, the father goes outside to his spaceship to hear the weather, but he presses the wrong button, and the spaceship takes off by mis-take. The worried family quickly puts on the weather report, which promises a pleasant day on Pluto.

BLOCKING OUT OF SCENES

Decide if you want a narrator and at which side of the screen he or she will sit. Rough out the important scenes (and who will be in them) that will move the story line *forward*. Al-ways focus on the dramatic question or problem (the suspense question) in your story; that is, who will win in watching the television show—the father or one of his children? Work out the narrator's script, which should be minimal, mainly tying scenes together. Make sure the dramatic question is solved by the protagonist (in this case, the father) or resolved through the action of the play's other characters.

REHEARSAL

This is an active time for exploration and experimenta-tion. Work on shadow mime; remember, it is how the charac-ter looks from the *side* that is the important factor. Keep the movement of the character applicable to that character. Find the right stroke in movement that will help define the charac-ter's emotions. Emotional states must be *shown* by the way the character sits, stands, moves, and uses his or her limbs. When adding costumes, remember it is the material showing up in shadow that is most important. Concentrate on contour and profile shapes—things that show up in outline. Always look at the shadow created—not the person—to see if the costume is correct.

After about a half hour of preparation, our improvisational production about the futuristic family really took off. Swirling stars, suns, and comets, along with electronic music, created the television screen. Different-colored gels added a mood of mystery and suspense. For the actual weather report, a cardboard with a Shazam cutout created the effect of flashing lightning as a sheet of tin simulated thunder in the background. Then the scene was transformed beautifully as the weather registered serenity and calm, reflected by soft lighting and music. Pairs of students behind the screen had opportunities to show different kinds of futuristic television programs, and the family had fun improvising in front of the screen.

An Arabian proverb states: "All sunshine makes a desert." Try some shadows in your life.

STORY THEATER

Story theater is a technique initiated and developed by Paul Sills. Paul Sills learned improvisational techniques early from his mother Viola Spolin, one of the founders of the improvisational movement in this country. Sills taught theater games when he was eighteen and went on to found a number of Chicago-based theater companies, including the Compass. The narrator-character device of story theater grew from the "Living Newspaper" format performed at the Compass during the late 1950s. There, Sills and his actors used newspaper stories as their dramatic text. The lines of the story were divided among the actors, who became the characters mentioned in the story. They performed actions associated with the character and setting described. For example, if the text said, "The President was on the golf course today, and ...," the actor playing the President actually said the line and could also mime playing golf, doffing his hat to a reporter, or some other associated action. These sketches, satirical in nature, were the beginnings of the technique in which characters—as part of the story—refer to themselves in the third person.

Sills has characterized story theater as ways of speaking with the body. The actors in this form depend a great deal on pantomime and body movement to capture and convey the essence of the story. Very minimal sets or props (or none at all) are used in story theater productions. Occasional sound effects and music are effectively utilized to suggest a mood or contribute to the play's atmosphere. The stage is essentially bare. The sense of space and time are effected through the use of actors as character-narrators. Each actor, in other words, narrates the story in the third person while enacting the part of one of the story's characters.

For example, at the start of the show, an actor might come out wearing tattered clothes and announce to the audience: "Once upon a time there lived a poor boy by the name of

Two scenes from Paul Sills's Story Theater: *The Golden Goose* starring Paul Sand and Valerie Harper; and *The Bremen Town Musicians*, starring Richard Schall and Richard Libertini as a rooster. Directed by Paul Sills and produced by Zev Bufman.

(*Photos by Steven Keull*)

Jack." A two- or three-piece combo off to one side of the stage might establish the appropriate atmosphere and mood by playing a peasant dance slowly and softly. The actor playing Jack continues the story: "One day, Jack was walking excitedly near his house, looking for his cow Bessie."

Thus, the actor starts the story as an objective narrator but at the same time assumes the characteristics of Jack. He might pantomime scooping up some hay and putting it into a bucket while looking for Bessie. The narrative line might continue: "Jack went in front of the house where Bessie was known to play." At this point an actress might enter and continue the story:

MOTHER: *Jack's mother was looking for her boy, as she had something very important to tell him.*

JACK: *And they bumped into each other.*

BESSIE: *Suddenly Bessie, the cow, entered and ran over to Jack. Kind of slow for a cow, you know. . . .*

(Here we might have some pantomime showing Jack petting his cow and the cow cuddling up to him.)

MOTHER: *Jack's mother marched up to him and said sadly: "Jack, we have to sell the cow right away."*

JACK: *Jack turned around and asked, "Why, Mother? I love Bessie very much."*

(Here we might pantomime giving Bessie some more hay from the mimed bucket he is carrying.)

Now the two actors, instead of continuing the narrative thread, could break into first-person dialogue.

MOTHER: *Jack, we are so poor. We need some money right away.*

JACK: *But Mother, how can we sell Bessie? I just can't do it.*

Eventually several other actors come onstage, each narrating parts of the story and acting roles in it. These actors assume their characters only after they have introduced themselves in the third person.

The shift between narrators and characters is effected through the process of transformation, discussed in Chapter 9. For example, in *Jack and the Beanstalk,* Jack leads the audience, so to speak, from a bare stage to a farm by assuming the physical qualities of a boy taking hay from a haystack and feeding a cow. Other actors might become the objects connected with a farm, such as trees, a small brook, or a pitchfork, à la fantasy mime (Chapter 6). A great deal of fluidity can be conveyed onstage by cutting through the time and space a narrative story might require. For example, on a page of any one particular story, a number of locales might be mentioned. In story theater, these changes are easily effected through the characters narrating this aspect, accompanied by the appropriate movement or pantomime. For example:

JACK: *So Jack slowly and sadly headed for the County Fair to sell Bessie* (Jack pantomimes walking around the stage, eventually crossing down stage), and *suddenly....*

BEAN SELLER: *He was greeted by a funny man carrying a strange bottle. Hi, there, young man! What's your name?*

JACK: *Jack, said Jack* (pause). *Jack was very curious, so he walked straight up to the man. Yes, sir?*

BEAN SELLER: *I am a magician, the funny man said. Would you like to see what I have in this bottle I am holding?*

JACK: *Yes, I would, said Jack.*

BEAN SELLER: *Here, then, take the bottle.*

JACK: *Jack took the bottle and opened it slowly.* (This is done in pantomime.) *Beans? It's only three beans!*

Later on in the play, the bean seller could easily become a new character or animal or even an inanimate object such as an oven in the Giant's home. A series of transformations may occur if there is a large cast of characters in the story, and doubling—even tripling—of characters is encouraged. In one of my workshops, the players were transformed into mice, then into horses, and then, moments later, blended in as people at the ball in *Cinderella.* In *Red Riding Hood,* they became part of the forest, chairs, and other props. In Sills's version of story theater, costume changes are suggested through body transformation and/or a simple change of headpiece. Ducky Daddles in the story of *Henny Penny*, for example, wears a baseball cap, and the Hen wears a red hat. The cat in *The Bremen Town Magicians* wears white gloves. A mouse could wear earmuffs, and so forth.

The advantage of story theater is that you can create many stage realities through simple dialogue and imaginative pantomime and movement. However, rigorous demands are made on individual actors as the primary, and often only vehicles for communicating the tale. Story theater is challenging but rewarding work for the actor. You must make the invisible concrete, leap imaginatively into many worlds, transform theatrical spaces, and come to trust the *simplicity* of the form yet be able and willing to experiment within that simplicity.

PUTTING ON A STORY THEATER PLAY
WITH YOUNG PEOPLE

1. The teacher or leader explains the technique of story theater—that the stories are essentially narrated and acted out at the same time. In order to make this narration and acting interesting, there will be ample opportunities for significant pantomime action that contributes either to characterization, the story, or the mood of the play.

2 The class and teacher (or cast and director) choose a story for dramatization. The story chosen should have lots of characters and a strong narrative and dramatic line. Good examples include *Jack and the Beanstalk, Henny Penny, Stone Soup, The Emperor's New Clothes, Jonah and the Whale, The Golden Goose, The Fisherman and His Wife, Joseph and His Brethren.* Skits can be anywhere from five to fifteen minutes long. Divide the class into small groups. After fifteen minutes of preparation, each group can improvise a short skit based on a familiar tale to see if the story theater form is correct.

3. Each rehearsal period should start off with loosening-up exercises and mime activity. Warm-up transformation games include passing around sounds and transforming them, passing around sounds and faces and transforming them, sound and motion transformations, mirror and distorted-mirror games.

4. Pantomime work should include action mime, such as miming simple activity (e.g., shoveling snow), an emotion (e.g., anger), a change of mood (e.g., putting on a scarf on a windy day), a character and walk (e.g., an infirm person crossing the street).

5. The story is read and reread, with players taking turns speaking lines.

6. Now the story is told in the words of the players. Play the game, Continuation Story, in which players take turns telling and miming the story for thirty seconds or so. Another good theater technique for story familiarization is gibberish.

7. Try on the characters after the parts are chosen or volunteered for, (try on miming the way the character walks); have two or three read the story while each of the players pantomimes the part. To familiarize the participants with the characters and stories use other good improvisational games, such as the magic scarf (Chapter 8) and sono-mime.

8. Break down the story in story theater format. For example, in *Jack and the Beanstalk,* the play might begin:

MOTHER (scrubbing the floor): *Once upon a time there was a poor widow.*

JACK (As he enters through an imaginary door): *Who had an only son named Jack.*

MILKY WHITE (trying to get in door as Mother closes it): *And a cow named Milky White.*

9. Review and discuss preparation for the parts, the *specific* personality traits and inner life of the characters: Jack is high-spirited but worried about the cow; the Mother is caring for Jack but strict under the circumstances; the Bean Seller is sly and conniving; and so forth.

10. Keep the staging simple. In most cases a bare stage with, perhaps, platforms and light projections will suffice. Much of the scenery can be made from the actors' bodies. For example, the players can pantomime rolling clouds, hills, the market stalls, the beanstalk that Jack climbs. Costumes, too, can be simple and imaginative. Remember, because the actor might be playing many characters, costumes should be flexible and not realistically rendered. For example, a long black coat for Foxy Woxy becomes a priest's habit for the Parson in *Henny Penny*.

Both for classroom and stage use, the simple, imaginative stroke will do, a stroke that conveys the larger whole. For the classroom, it is a good idea to keep a costume scrap box from which you can adapt clothing at hand. For example, leftover tapestries, fancy draperies, and discarded curtains can be adapted to the needs of the show. Crepe paper, crinkled newspaper, oilcloth (for "leather" trimmings), and burlap (which, when redone with silver paint, makes excellent plate armor) can be used for costuming. Belts can be made from tagboard or felt; crowns can be constructed from gilded tag or cardboard made from felt. Sandals can be made by tying laces around the legs and bare feet. The simplest materials treated imaginatively can transform the ordinary into the beautiful, as

The Patchwork Players performing a story theater fable.
(*Photo by Alex Gersznowicz*)

when cheesecloth is turned into lace and dyed-out cotton flannel becomes velvet.

For more permanent costuming in a stage presentation, a designer works with the director and set designer to ensure that all the visual elements work together in a harmonious whole.

In their musical mime *Hot Headlines*, the CoMixCo cast wore hot-colored blouses and scarves to complement the newspaper collage backdrop. The Patchwork Players wore single patches on their jeans, colored blouses, and suspenders—to complement the setting of large patchwork squares.

11. Prepare a final working script. Break it down into scenes. For example:

- Jack sells cow to peddler for magic beans.
- Mother throws foolish beans away.
- Beans begin to grow.
- Vine grows. Jack climbs it.
- Jack searches Giant's house, protected by Giant's wife.
- Finds Golden Goose and steals it.
- Jack climbs down vine, pursued by Giant.
- Giant in hot pursuit down vine after Jack.
- Jack chops down vine.
- Giant falls off and dies.
- Golden egg from goose makes Jack and Mother rich.

12. Make a final selection of cast and crew. Encourage doubling of parts. Other participants can be chosen as a stage manager, costume designers and crew, set designers and crew, prompters. Think about the possibility of chorus and musical accompaniment. Original songs can be written. Some songs can be adapted. For example, one class at P.S. 50 in Manhattan that performed *Snow White* had the dwarves enter singing a favorite rock song about knocking on the ceiling three times if help were needed.

SUGGESTIONS FOR STAGING
IN STORY THEATER

STAGE GEOGRAPHY

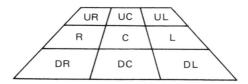

STAGE POSITIONS

The following are *general* considerations, and directorial decisions must always be made according to what is *specifically* happening during each moment of the play's action in terms of character delineation, composition, and focus.

1. Down right is usually the best spot for direct narration.
2. Down center is the best spot for high points of the play, but this position should be used sparingly.
3. Down left is generally good for scenes of tension.
4. Up right is generally good for eavesdropping and intrigue.
5. Up center is generally good for scenes of royalty, authority, and dignity.

Generally speaking, the following are the strongest (starting with 1) positions onstage:

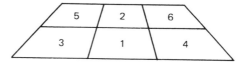

However, stage positions must always be considered in terms of what is *specifically* happening at each moment in the story, character delineation, composition, and focus.

ALTERNATIVE STAGING

The typical school play is usually given in a large room with a small proscenium stage, making it difficult for the audiences of young people to see or hear well. The experience

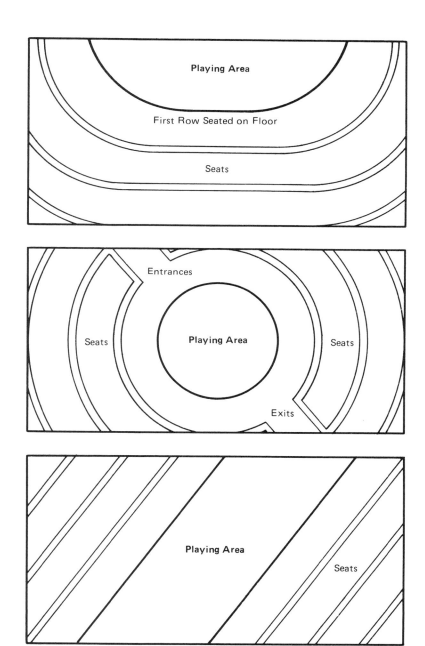

First row is seated on floor.
Staggered rows of seats can be placed behind.

usually turns out to be a discipline problem for the teacher and a frightening one for the players.

Audiences, as well as players, can be more involved and relaxed if some of the following alternative staging plans are used.

THEATER TERMS

You may wish to acquaint players with the following terms:

- *Cross*—move to another player.

- *Cross above*—move upstage.

- *Cross below*—move downstages of player.

- *Open up*—turn to audience.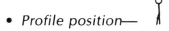

- *Turn out*—less of body to audience.

- *Profile position*—

- *Full position*—

- *Three-quarter position*—

- *Focus*—look at another player.

- *Cover*—do not stand in front of another player.

- *Dress the stage*—keep the stage picture in balance. Notice in the following diagram that Player C crosses to Player A and Player B "dresses the stage."

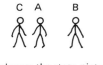

(B balances the stage picture)

1   2   3

If the play is to be done for audiences, the following questions may prove useful to the leader for evaluating stage composition and movement:

1. Are the players' faces clearly *visible* to the audience except when deliberately hidden?
2. Do the players *move naturally* from one stage picture to the next?
3. Does each stage picture have a *center of attention* or clear focus?
4. Is there *variety* in visual composition onstage?
5. Does each *stage grouping* help to tell the story?
6. Does the *center of attention* onstage generally include the speaking player(s)?
7. Is there *variety* in standing, sitting, and lying positions?
8. Is there *variety* in body positions—open, closed, profile, and so on? Have you avoided repeating the same movement too often? (Try for maximum variety for the eye. Avoid having the players lined up in straight lines or lining up in a semicircle around one particular player.)
9. Are all movements onstage *motivated*?
10. Do the movements either help to *delineate character, hold attention,* or *explain character relationships*?

VALUES OF STORY THEATER

The form of story theater stresses simplicity, spontaneity, and fluidity. The point of story theater is to revive the central importance of storytelling, which has kept the theater so vital through the ages, while connecting with interests of contemporary audiences. On Broadway and elsewhere, story theater has dramatized narrative works of literature, including folktales and fairy tales, fables and history.

Story theater helps to make what could be a task into a joy. Reading material becomes interesting and exciting; what's more, it is chosen by the participants themselves. "Book-

279

Contemporary tales can be told in Story Theater form.
(*Photo by Alex Gersznowicz*)

shelves," wrote one classroom teacher, "began to fill up with every fairy tale, fable, or legend the children could get their hands on after trying out Story Theater." The integral learning phases of reading, oral expression, and written expression are combined in the class. Freedom of expression and confidence are enhanced. Wrote the teacher: "Our work in pantomime games and improvisational techniques certainly paid off when I saw how beautifully the children brought each character alive and the freedom and exhilaration they showed in doing it."

The excitement of mounting a play onstage or for an assembly program motivates learning. Story theater is one activity where the values of improvisation for school and stage are truly integrated. One teacher, Carole Rosen, remarked:

Besides inspiring an eager desire to learn to read and write, doing Story Theater helped the children to enjoy coming to school to share ideas. They were no longer pre-

*occupied with fighting and acting out aggressively to re-
lease their tensions. They found a more profitable way to
express their emotions. The crowning achievement I feel
worth noting was made by a boy who was a serious behavior problem from the minute he entered school, re-
fused to do any work in class at all, could not read above
the second grade level, and whose mother admitted he
was certainly on his way to reform school. After he found
his niche as the Little Grey Man in* The Golden Goose, *he
did his first written work of the year,* The Wizard of Oz.

Original story theater skits may also be devised, as long as the
stories have a simple, yet strong, dramatic line.

SUGGESTIONS FOR ORIGINAL STORY THEATER SKITS
1. An odyssey adventure (e.g., a trip around the world)
2. A detective story (e.g., people on a subway—who pulled
   the cord?)
3. Animals taking over a pet store
4. Toys coming alive in a department store
5. "You Were There"—recreation of historical events
6. Contrasting living and nonliving things
7. Animals in and out of their environments
8. The worlds of play/sports/work
9. Holidays around the world
10. Family and community roles.

Add your own:

_____

_____

_____

We hope your journey into the world of improvisation
has been fun and worthwhile. We know it is a journey that has

A Farewell Machine comprised by members of the Summer Institute of Drama for Teachers directed by Milton Polsky.
(*Photo by W. H. Edwards*)

only really begun, because the contents of this book can be explored in a continuing process of rediscovery.

We trust that you have discovered many things about yourself and others while becoming more aware of your body, your senses, and the creative powers of your imagination. The theme of this book can now be restated simply. It is fun to buy a valentine, more fun to make one, and perhaps the most fun to actually become one. How much more rewarding it is to see not only with your eyes but with your whole body—to become so many different things, people, and places that you can let yourself go with the assurance and confidence that comes with discovery, exploration, and training.

"It is possible to fly without motors, but not without knowledge and skills." So wrote one of the Wright brothers, the inventors of the first heavier-than-air airplanes. He might have added, as he himself proved, that imagination helps too. May yours continue to soar in the wonderful worlds of improvisation.

282

The On-the-Spot Players make a giant airplane in "Flying" number during *Celebration* performance; choreography by Shelley Gail Weiss-Lightman.
(*Photo by Leonard Lewis*)

PLAYER'S DIARY

1. What is your favorite movie? When you see it again, look for examples of improvisations, and record the images.

2. What is your favorite musical? Do you recall any improvisation in it? If so, describe what you saw.

3. What is your favorite play? Do you recall if the characters improvised any action in it?

4. Record the different kinds of shadows you observe during the day and evening.

5. What kinds of shadows did you enjoy performing in mime?

6. What is your favorite shadow theater activity?

7. What is your favorite fairy tale, legend, or fable? Do you think it lends itself to story theater? Why?

8. What character did you most enjoy portraying in story theater?

9. What character from all the exercises in this book did you most enjoy enacting?

10. What was your favorite exercise in this book? Why?

Add your own questions, thoughts, and observations.

APPENDIXES

APPENDIX A: THE LEADER'S ROLE

The leader may be a teacher, stage director, or anyone conducting a particular session or exercise within a session of improvisational drama. The role of any leader in creative group endeavors is to inspire, motivate, and guide participants so that they can best actualize their own creativity.

In improvisational drama, an important role of the leader is to be a situation provider, knowing full well that stimuli for genuine creativity lies within each player's experience. The creative leader helps the participants to look inside themselves and see what they can build from their own imaginations. In guiding, the leader helps participants to be aware of and open to new impressions, recognizing each participant as unique.

KNOWING THE GROUP

A caring leader is constantly aware of the changing interests and needs of a particular group. This takes work, but the search and process of discovery in drama, luckily, are creative endeavors. Observing the group will in itself yield valuable insight concerning likes, dislikes, favorite activities, story appeals, and personal backgrounds as well as social and political insights, childhood memories, and current concerns.

In addition to directly observing the participants in actual play, talk with them about their interests, experiences, life-styles, and needs. Share with them, for example, what they consider the ten worst problems in the world, their favorite and unfavorite characters, what they would be or do if they had a choice in the matter. Learn to accept strong feelings, even if they do not square with your values and perceptions of life.

Good leadership also entails sensing that evaluation is a creative process. Try not to impose your own interpretation unless it is requested by a group. You may, however, encourage constructive evaluation of what worked, what didn't work, and what parts of a scene or play can be improved. Remember, the process of revision and refinement and the shaping of any impulse is intended to give the player's creative energy a focus and framework. Do not take over what others have started. Try, as humanly as possible, to be authoritative without being authoritarian, to be a guide and not a god—in short, to be a creative director and never a dictator.

UNDERSTANDING GOALS: PROCESS AND PRODUCT

Creativity has been characterized as elaborated insight, the shaping and transformation of impulses and impressions into new concepts, perceptions, and forms of expression. How much and how far an improvisational exercise is to be shaped and refined always depends upon the degree of and for whom the communication is intended.

Improvisational drama can be considered primarily for the benefit of the players themselves—for personal and social awareness and growth—a way of exploring new roles and redefining old roles; experimenting with problem solving, dramatic conflict, and learning to become more aware of self and others through social interaction; expressing themselves for the sake of their own creative needs.

Leaders and players may value spontaneity for its own intrinsic merit and not wish really to refine an exercise for an audience. On the other hand, any number of exercises found in this book can become the basis for a product to be refined and rehearsed for an audience in a school, community, or recreation center.

HELPING TO PREPARE

A creative leader recognizes the importance of revision and realizes that playing without planning leads to chaos but that often, over-planning can kill spontaneity and freshness. Quick flashes of insight can always be elaborated on, depending on the degree of communication intended. A balance often evolves between conscious deliberation about a problem and the spontaneous combustion of ideas that occurs during the planning, play, and evaluation stages.

PROVIDING STIMULI

Whether an improvisation is done for only a few moments a day for pure creative enjoyment or as part of a group-created scene or an individual improv, stimuli are needed to start the wheels of the imagination turning. The imaginative leader comes prepared with such stimuli but is also wide open to the contributions of workshop members. The stimuli can be sights, sounds, music, words, objects (real and imaginary), colors, pictures, props, poems, or stories as suggested in this text and contributed by the players.

GUIDING DEVELOPMENT AND REFINEMENT

In addition to being a situation provider, one of the primary goals of good leadership is to provide cues from which the players can make discoveries of their own. You will spark more creativity if you ask evocative questions instead of making statements of what you would like to see. After setting up a basic improvisation, provide cues for the players themselves to discover their characters. Avoid saying, for example: "I want you to be an angry customer in a shoe store." It is better to ask the player: "What are you doing in the shoe store?" What do you want as the character? How do you feel about it?"

GUIDING FOR EVALUATION

As evaluation guideposts, you might, for example, ask such questions as: Could you really believe in what you as the characters were doing—were your actions motivated? How much of the story will be reworked and refined? In other words, how can a situation or scene be improved, so that the players *themselves* discover and see what must be improved? Encourage the players to conduct their own evaluation and feedback sessions, centering on awareness issues such as the following:

1. Did the group show imagination? *Specifically* how?
2. Did the group show teamwork? *Specifically* how?
3. Give *examples* of how the group communicated its efforts.

Then the group can zero in on feedback for the specific activity at hand, following and varying guidelines found throughout this book.

GROWING IN GROUPS

Through interaction with other players, an individual is most likely to become less inhibited and more expressive. She or he gains confidence in creative and thinking abilities when interacting positively with others and thus becomes more confident. Players learn the important lesson of holding one another's attentive interest. Self-confidence, in turn, helps the communication process with others.

Groups also grow when they can share close relationships based on mutual exploration of skills and new art forms. In improvisational drama, players will learn from each other in the process of working on an open-ended but *concrete* problem dealing with human conflict. A beautiful irony of improvisational activity is that people—to discover and imaginatively resolve confrontation—must work together, create together, and—through this process—learn from one another.

Cooperative interaction in improvisational drama groups does not happen all at once. Groups need a chance to grow, to generate their own intrinsic contributions to the whole. Players need encouragement and a sense of success—things that you, as a leader, can help generate by helping to provide a warm, supportive environment. What the players create will, in most cases, come from their collective and individual experience, so it can never be really "wrong." It may be merely something you did not have in mind. Therefore, it is worth repeating: It is important for you never to impose your ideas on the work of the group or individual concerned. If this happens, not only is the joy of the creative process taken away, but the players are also cheated out of the meaningful learning experience of thinking through a problem and experimenting with a solution.

WORKING TOGETHER

A sense of unity will promote a group's desire for success, and in this respect, success means working together.

It is important to avoid cliques—which will often evolve in an intimate group setting—so as to give everybody an opportunity to contribute during creation of the situations, skits, and plays. To foster social growth—the players' getting to know one another a bit better through sharing their common tasks—the system of randomization is suggested. How it works is discussed next.

FORMING SUBGROUPS

Based on the number of smaller groups needed, everyone in the larger group counts off at random up to the number of groups needed until everyone has a number. For example, say five subgroups are needed. Going around a circle, everyone counts off: 1, 2, 3, 4, 5; 1, 2, 3, 4, 5; then all the 1s, all the 2s, all the 3s, all the 4s, all the 5s meet together in different parts of the room. They are now ready to receive instructions about the problem at hand and to prepare and create.

This method is not as impersonal as it may appear. Randomization prevents bickering over who will play with whom and puts the emphasis on the creative fun itself. You may wish to explain to the workshop members why you are using this method, a common procedure in any informal workshop. Through frequently randomizing your workshop into different combinations of participants, each player will effectively get to know others who are different— whether it be in race, sex, background, interests, or intelligence— because a common bond will develop from solving the particular improvisational problem at hand.

TIPS FOR SUCCESSFUL GROUP WORK

1. Plan the activities of your session(s) carefully. Block out your work. Allow enough time for preparation, and come prepared to lead.

2. Instruct clearly. Be sure the groups know what is expected of them. Make sure each session has a *focus* of attention and a *framework* for development.

289

3. Guide, energize, and support beginning groups until they feel confident to work independently. Be aware that although a clear *focus* can lead to creative *flow*, it often works the other way around: creative flow can lead to a more clearly defined *focus* and *framework*. Be flexible with structure.

4. Be sure the size of each subgroup is right for the particular task.

5. Rules can be creative, too. Players themselves need and often request structures and help in organization. Well-focused discipline channels the direction of the creative experience.

Good luck with your program and creative leadership! And remember: Always expect the unexpected, but never be unprepared.

APPENDIX B: HALLOWEEN HAPPENING

SCENARIO

Greetings

Meet kids at door, and bring them to circle. One of us to at least one kid. Kids will be wearing name tags (in shape of pumpkins). We will all be Spirits, dressed in black and orange combinations with masks (optional). (Tell them we're going to have a party.) Settle them down, tell about us, and ask about them. *Great Spirit* enters, welcomes them, and announces that the *Great Goblin* will be coming later with a Yummy Surprise. (*5 minutes*)

Warm-Up; Move When the Spirit Says Move!

Need: Instruments, piano, drum, etc. Shake, hop, wiggle, etc. (Prepare some one-word directions in advance.) Ask kids for *their* ideas too. Stay in circle, standing. (*5 minutes*)

Quiet Pantomime: Balloon Game

Need: Piano music. 15–20 orange/black balloons. Situations written on orange construction paper. Everyone prepare two situations. Keep them short (one sentence) with a definite action written in. (*10 minutes*) For example:

- You are a witch flying on a broomstick.
- You are a cat drinking from a bowl of milk.

Pass the balloons around in a circle until the music stops. Burst the balloons with a pin. The children then act out their situations.

Story Theater Skit

With audience involvement from kids, sounds, echoes, etc. (*5 minutes*)

Pantomime Pictures to Act Out

Need: The pictures, Scotch tape. Who supplies pictures? On wall? (*5–10 minutes*)

Choral Reading

In different part of room. Need: Candles (*black and orange*) or flashlight. (*5 minutes*)

Spirit Sez
Take leads from kids' costumes (e.g., Spirit Sez move like Snoopy; be strong like Superman, etc.) (*5 minutes*)

Shadow Skits—3
Talk over and refine in your groups; decide on order.

Songs
Go over and rehearse such songs as "Going to the Scare-In" (variation of "Going to Kentucky").

Refreshments and Farewells
At door with *Great Goblin*.

APPENDIX C: HOT HEADLINES

SCENARIO

Opener
Sono-montage. Actor, carrying newspaper, enters bare stage and reacts to newspaper by making an expressive sound (such as *ooh*); one by one the rest of the cast comes out, picks up the preceding sound, and transforms it, creating a mosaic of sounds in counterpoint. The newspaper is then laid down, and the leader transforms an imaginary newspaper into a mimed object such as a rope or ball, followed by the transformation into a succession of other objects. The cast members now find themselves in a subway, reading newspapers, the music developing into a rock sound as the ensemble sings the title song that concludes:

> *. . . so if you're down in the dumps*
> *and haven't a thing to do . . .*
> *just pick up the paper and read it*
> *the whole day through . . .*
> *Hot Headlines!*

Weather Report
Two actors (hereafter referred to as *elicitors*) evoke from the audience suggestions as to what kinds of weather they like. Small groups from the ensemble take turns producing sun, rain, snow (etc.) machines, interconnected through body and sound.

On-the-Spot News Interviews
Elicitors ask audience for a "face and a place" from storyland, history, television, etc. Short skits are improvised, incorporating the famous personality and place, such as the mayor being interviewed by Mickey Mouse in a launderette.

Horoscopes
Actors individually mime or sing about key traits of the zodiac signs. Elicitors briefly talk about characteristics of the horoscopes and then ask members of the audience their zodiac signs. Two signs are selected at a time. Actors (after a short huddle to plan the skit) mime a situation that could happen between them while two other actors on the sidelines supply their voices. The vocalizers might sing

operatically, use amusing accents, or direct the actors to move in slow motion.

Angry Letters to the Editor

Elicitors ask the audience who makes them angry. Depending on responses (such as mother, father, friend, teacher, brother), actors—in combinations of two—prepare a short, humorous skit in which the emotional feelings are expressed in gibberish.

Lost and Found

Elicitors ask for a lost object and a found object. Using a story narrator, a story is enacted in which all the props are made by the actors' bodies. For example, the actors become chairs, swinging doors, animals, and other objects including the lost and found ones suggested by the audience.

Finale

Actors do a closing variation of opening sono-montage and end up with rousing reprise of "Hot Headlines."

During the actual performances, suggestions from the audience and the actors' own creative interplay provided a spontaneous, exciting show for all.

An alternative format is a "Saturday Night Live" take-off. After a mirror warm-up, the ensemble makes a group machine consisting of the sights and sounds of a TV studio. The group sings "Welcome to the Studio," a variation of "Welcome to the Theater" (Appendix E). Then the audience provides a "face and a place" for a celebrity in the news—three-person Gibberviews; "As the World Twists and Turns" comes next, performed in two's and three's. This segment is followed by a closer look "Behind the Scenes" (players given hidden thoughts of newsmakers in variations on sono-mime). The audience-participation show concludes with the audience providing choices for endings in "What Do You Do?" musical skits performed in a variety of theater styles (Chapter 11).

APPENDIX D: TOURING COMPANY

SCENARIO

You're sitting in your seat (school, college, hospital). Suddenly a space lights up, and a troupe of players enter, snappily singing and dancing to "Wash Your Linen!"

> *In this world of rising taxes*
> *Broken hearts and changing sexes*
> *It may seem that you just can't win. . . .*

Right before your eyes, the company sets up white sheets and props and, through movement and sound, magically transforms the playing area into a public laundromat, where all kinds of characters from the community are likely to congregate.

> *But we got the tonic*
> *For a new kind of gin*
> *A public washing of the times*
> *We live in. . . .*

For the next forty-five minutes or so, there unfolds a musical revue of songs and skits dealing with social matters of concern to the audience—from teenage dating to the uses and abuses of nuclear power. Drama can play an important role in enlightening people about *specific* pressing issues of the day. Who can they turn to for help? What can they themselves do? How can society become more aware of its role and responsibilities? The purpose of the tour is to explore these and other particular questions in dramatic form. *And it will be done in a way that encourages the audience to become a vital part of the show.*

The manager of the laundromat invites members of the audience to join the scene onstage, or *through suggestions from their seats,* to change the direction of the scene. Just as the touring playing space has been changed into a laundromat, so too is the laundromat transformed into many different kinds of worlds where the action unfolds. The audience involvement follows this pattern:

- Ensemble elicits ideas for skit.
- Song (and dance) introducing skit.
- Skit/variations.

WASH YOUR LINEN

Words by
JAIMEY STEELE and
MILTON POLSKY

Music by
JAIMEY STEELE

For example:

- The ensemble asks an audience of senior adults: "Where would you like to go, if you could go anywhere? (Suppose the responses include Florida.)
- Song "Flying" (written by Aaron Lightman):

  Flying . . .
  To Florida (any place can be substituted)
  It's sunny every day
  And it (almost) never snows
  The gentle breeze is soft
  And it always blows. . . .

- In this case, the skit concerns a retired couple visiting "idyllic" Miami. They have worked hard all their lives to save some money and now are victims of a con game involving the sale of property (or perhaps theft of their traveler's checks).

The action of the scripted skit is flexible and stops periodically to allow for the spontaneous changing of characters and circumstances. Thus within a ten-minute skit the *audience* would play a significant part in *selecting* and *seeing* various problems enacted (both negative and positive role models) and in *discussing* the particular consequences of their choices of stage behavior.

The audience will always have opportunities—through examination of their experiences and extension of their imaginations—to *affect the choice* of the people, place, and plot.

The show's structure assumes this shape:

1. "Wash your linen"—opening song and dance, setting up of environment of the show
2. "Life Is Like a Bar of Soap"—song, intro to troubles encountered—life problems
3. Elicit for skit—(where you from?)
4. "Let's Put (name of hometown, school, etc.) on Broadway" (song with bouncing ball on sheet, serving as intro to skit 1)
5. *Skit 1* (e.g., reality of inflation/variations)
6. Elicit for Skit 2—(where would you like to be?)
7. "Flying"—song and dance (human bird with sheet, intro to skit 2)

8. *Skit 2* (ideal solutions/variations)

9. Elicit for Skit 3—(what would happen if you won the lottery?)

10. "If I Won the Lottery"—song and dance, intro to skit 3

11. *Skit 3* (inflation fantasy/variations—use sheet for shadow play)

12. "Makes Dollars and Sense"—song in skit 3, dealing with self-awareness and responsibility

13. "No Laughing Matter"—final song, dealing with responsibilities of society

There can also be discussion (aided by representatives from an appropriate agency) at the end of the show based on audience reactions.

APPENDIX E: BASIC FORMAT FOR AUDIENCE PARTICIPATION SHOW

"CELEBRATION"—THE ON-THE-SPOT PLAYERS

"Spotters"*	What	Who	Audience Involvement
Milt	Song: "Out of the Morning" Mirrors: Body Transformations Song: "Welcome to the Theatre"	All	None
Brenda	International Greeting Machine	All	Specific countries
Amy G. Abby	Song: "Flying" Gibberviews	Teams of three	Countries Questions
Paul Amanda	Twists and Turns	All (in groups of two)	Conflicts Home/School/ Job
Tracy Elinor	Create-a-World	All	First World First Person
Louise Meryl	Song: "Coney Island"— beach skits	All	Things to do at the beach
Paul	Finale: International Farewell Machine Curtain call	All	None

* Spotters introduce section and elicit requests from audience.

WELCOME TO THE THEATER

Words and Music by
AARON LIGHTMAN,
JAIMEY STEELE and
MILTON POLSKY

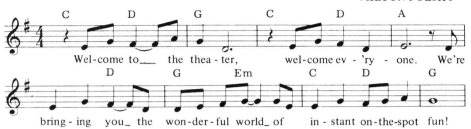

Wel-come to_ the thea - ter, wel-come ev - 'ry - one. We're
bring - ing you_ the won-der - ful world_ of in - stant on-the-spot fun!

APPENDIX F: SAMPLE SCENARIO OF IMPROVISATIONAL PLAY

PANDORA'S BOX
BY MILTON POLSKY & JOAN GARDNER

Scene	*Who*	*What*	*Where*
1.	Chaos, Jupiter, and Clouds	Jupiter's intention to create a peaceful place after witnessing chaos.	Mt. Olympus & Space
2.	Jupiter, Gods, and Environments	Jupiter creates rivers, forests, fish, animals.	Earth & Mt. Olympus
3.	Jupiter and Epimetheus	Jupiter creates Man from fire, earth, air, and water—sends him down to Earth. Epimetheus asks for companionship.	Mt. Olympus & Earth
4.	Jupiter and Pandora	Jupiter creates Pandora from the elements.	Mt. Olympus
5.	Gods,)Goddesses, and Pandora	Gifts given to Pandora and warning by Jupiter not to open box.	Mt. Olympus
6.	Mercury, Pandora, and Epimetheus	Mercury brings Pandora to Earth and introduces her to Epimetheus.	Space & Earth

Scene	Who	What	Where
7.	Epimetheus, Pandora, and Environments	Epimetheus introduces her to the beauties of Earth.	Earth
8.	Pandora	She hears voice from the box and opens it.	Earth
9.	Pandora, Plagues, and Evils	Plagues and Evils escape from box and cover Earth.	Garden & Earth
10.	People, Animals, and Fish	Know disease and despair for the first time.	Earth & Sea
11.	Jupiter (Epimetheus and Pandora)	Orders Pandora away.	Mt. Olympus & Earth
12.	Epimetheus, Pandora, and Hope	He leaves to hunt for food; Pandora finds Hope.	Earth

APPENDIX G: USES OF IMPROVISATION TO INVESTIGATE SCRIPTED CHARACTERS

In scripted plays creative improvisation can be an effective tool in a variety of rehearsal experiences, ranging from auditions and casting to investigating characters already created by a playwright. Through improvisation, you can explore the past life, inner life, and offstage life of a scripted character as well as help solve technical problems related to characterization.

It has been said that the essence of good acting, as well as good living, is the discovery of the next moment in all its fullness. Because improvisation requires intense observation, concentration, and the spontaneous freeing of the imagination, you can more effectively probe the emotional life of a character and help to insure a freshness of the "here and now" quality so vital to the theater by applying the techniques in this book to the creation of *any* character, silent or verbal. Improvisation helps directors and actors to explore beneath and between the character's lines of dialogue.

Improvisation as an audition technique can be immensely useful. For example, a number of directors ask those trying out for a play to enact a creative movement or verbal improvisation to get an idea of an actor's imaginative potential. They find that an improvisation with the potential to open up the imagination can reveal far more than just a cold or even a prepared reading from a script. Many good possibilities for the right person for a part are overlooked when a director relies only on a reading. Some actors who give what appears to be a terrific reading at an audition and consequently get the part may never progress in their comprehension and communication of the role beyond that reading. On the other hand, only fair readers, who for some reason or other foul up at a reading, may grow immeasurably during the course of rehearsals. Granted, these are extremes, but in both cases some improvisational work may give the director better clues concerning the actor's true potential. Once a cast is chosen, our actors usually do not really start to investigate the script until they have related the life of the characters to their own lives through improvisation. The content of these improvisations, in turn, may be recalled later in rehearsal as the actors personalize more and get more into their parts. Of course, the amount of time that can be spent on improvisations depends on the kind of play one is doing and how much time can be allotted to it along with other investigative methods during rehearsal. Often, even a few minutes of improvisational work can unblock a particular problem or give added insight into what a character is thinking or feeling.

THE PAST LIFE

A character may become more meaningful if, instead of merely discussing those past events that influence the current life of the character, the director could ask, for example, the actor playing George in *Who's Afraid of Virginia Woolf?* to recreate the scene with his father-in-law (who does not actually appear in the play), where the father-in-law tries to block George's novel from being published. Dramatizing and recreating in mime a scene where there is a supposed boxing match between the two men helps to clarify the ambivalent fears George has about his wife and his own feelings of suppressed rage and submerged hopes and doubts.

As another example, in *The Country Girl* by Clifford Odets, the husband and wife, to comprehend their present relationship better, could improvise the scene where he finds her drunk in bed; or her early life on a farm could be dramatized in contrast to her present married life to an actor in a large, overpopulated, depersonalizing city.

While rehearsing *A Raisin in the Sun,* Barbara Endelman, a player and teacher, took her high school students back in a time capsule to five years before the play begins, when Ruth and Walter Younger are still discovering each other in the early years of their marriage. Beneatha, Walter's sister, has not yet begun to experience her generation gap problems. Travis is a very young boy. All their goals seem obtainable, for the pressure of the insurance money Momma Younger is to receive in the course of the play is not a problem yet. In this exercise, the characters improvised how they would have reacted to each other and pantomimed what they would have done as they escape from the time capsule one by one. This silent improvisation helped to clarify the way the characters felt about each other at the end of the play when they were once more reunited as a family.

THE OFFSTAGE LIFE

Offstage life, those events that are referred to in the script but never actually seen, or those events that might occur between scenes of the play, when recreated improvisationally, help the actor get closer

305

to the role. For example, in *The Glass Menagerie,* Tom refers to going to the movies all the time to escape the harsh and boring reality of his existence. A pantomime can be done with Tom secretly getting dressed to go to the movies, so that his emotions and thoughts are revealed through how he feels and how he reacts because of those feelings. The actor playing Tom might become aware of tiny thought patterns by exploring his emotions and physical life and projecting those actions while waiting in line at the movies.

A similar improvisation from this Tennessee Williams classic might be Laura dressing for her "date" with the gentleman caller, a friend from Tom's job, whom Tom, under pressure from Amanda, has asked home for dinner.

In Arthur Miller's *Death of a Salesman,* the actor playing Willy Loman might portray physically the exhaustion of this salesman as he drives miles, yet sells very little on one of those hot summer days.

THE POST LIFE

An awareness of a character's emotional or physical life, objective, or relationship to other characters might be determined by the director and an actor if future events, based upon what happens in the play, are considered and created improvisationally. For example, *Go Bid the Soldiers Shoot* might be a title for a mime play inspired by Shakespeare's *Hamlet.* A continuation of the play's struggle between Fortinbras and Horatio might develop when the company of players within the drama proper recreate some of the scenes from the play that are variously interpreted by Fortinbras and Horatio. A power struggle between Fortinbras and Horatio ensues, thus providing an insight and a physical awareness of how all the characters involved in this improvisation might react in other events, including the dramatic moments in *Hamlet.*

Any story or play's post life certainly helps the actors stretch their imaginations to get inside the parts they are portraying. In this respect, you can explore with both adults and young people the afterlife of a number of stories with surprising results. Do Cinderella and the Prince really live happily ever after? In one group, the usually passive Cinderella started to challenge her husband's traditional authority and asserted her own sense of integrity and uniqueness. In a version by another group, Cinderella rejected the Prince's hand in marriage and instead decided to live with the magical wizard, who replaced the traditional fairy godmother. She decided to become a journalist to tell the true story of her experience, her new-found occupation beautifully captured improvisationally. All you need to ask is "what really happened?" for some insightful probes not only into the characters but into the lives of the players themselves. Try some new ending-beginnings yourself.

Add your own:

_____

_____

_____

ADDITIONAL SUGGESTIONS

1. Write or draw your impressions of your scripted character according to the following categories: *adjectives* (how many different ones describe your character at different times?); *colors* (including subtle nuances); *animals* (or fish or fowl); *dramatic function* (hero, confidant, foil, etc.); *goals and obstacles and lifestyle* (habits, environment, dress, etc.).

2. In a circle, everyone discusses his or her lifestyle, paying attention to as many details as possible.

3. Now everyone, *in character*, discusses the lifestyle of his or her scripted character.

4. Players walk (in character) to a blackboard, if handy, and sign their characters' names. (If an argument erupts between characters, say between Antigone and Lucy van Pelt, stay in character.) Now, on the board, write the adjectives that best describe your character.

5. Imagine your character is attending a cocktail party. Everyone walks around the space designated as the party. At different intervals, carry on a conversation with another character. At different times, become your character's animal or color and carry on a conversation with another character.

6. Change the party space to a different locale (hospital, North Pole, etc.) and carry on conversation with another character. Add an element of conflict.

7. Stay in character for at least one hour in the morning and evening during your normal weekly or week-end school, work, or leisure activity.

8. As yourself—and, as your scripted character, record in your diary—how you felt about the above experience. Talk about it with the other players.

9. Enact a sono-mime to express the inner feelings of your scripted character.

10. As your scripted character, try some of the exercises in this book and talk about or write down your feelings. As your scripted character, make up an improvisational exercise or vary one found in *Let's Improvise!*

BIBLIOGRAPHY

Courtney, Richard. *Play, Drama and Thought.* London: Cassell, 1968.

Davis, Flora. *Inside Intuition: What We Know about Nonverbal Communication.* New York: McGraw-Hill, 1971.

Dewey, John. "The Aims of History in Elementary Education," *The School and Society.* Chicago: University of Chicago Press, 1915.

Ducharte, Pierre Louis. *The Italian Comedy.* New York: Harper & Row, 1929.

Gordon, Mel. "Foregger and the Dance of the Machines," *The Drama Review,* Vol. 19, No. 1 (March 1975), p. 72.

Hale, Pat, ed. *Participation Theatre for Young Audiences.* New York: New Plays for Children, 1972.

Hamilton, Edith. *Mythology.* New York: Mentor Books, New American Library, 1942.

Jones, Robert Edmond. *The Dramatic Imagination.* New York: Duell, Sloan and Pearce, 1941.

Kalem, T. E., "Allegorical Romp," *Time,* November 9, 1970, p. 48.

Lewis, Howard R. and Streitfeld, Harold S. *Growth Games*. New York: Harcourt Brace Jovanovich, 1970.

Lorayne, Harry and Lucas, Jerry. *The Memory Book*. New York: Ballantine Books, 1974.

Marceau, Marcel. *The Marcel Marceau Alphabet Book*. New York: Doubleday, 1970 (Produced by George Mendoza).

Oreglio, G. *Commedia dell' Arte*. New York: Hill and Wang, 1968.

Peterson, Severin, ed. *A Catalog of the Ways People Grow*. New York: Ballantine Books, 1971.

Polsky, Milton and Gardner, Joan. *Pandora's Box: Creata-Play Learning Kit*. New York: Cal Press, 1975; Westwood Press, 1978.

Roberts, Vera Mowry. *On Stage*. New York: Harper & Row, 1962.

Sandburg, Carl. *The Wedding Procession of the Rag Doll and the Broom Handle Who Was in It*. New York: Harcourt Brace Jovanovich, 1922; A & W Publishers, 1979.

Severn, Richard. *Shadow Magic: The Story of Shadow Play*. New York: David McKay, 1959.

Simon, Sidney B., Howe, Leland W. and Kirschenbaum, Howard. *Values Clarification: A Handbook of Practical Strategies for Teachers and Students*. New York: Hart Publishing, 1972; 1978.

Spolin, Viola. *Improvisation for the Theatre*. Chicago: Northwestern University Press, 1963.

Sypher, Wylie, ed. *Comedy*. Garden City, N.Y.: Doubleday Anchor Books, 1956.

Teasdale, Sara. *Collected Poems of Sara Teasdale*. New York: Macmillan, 1920.

Way, Brian. *Development through Drama*. New York: Humanities Press, 1967.

INDEX